Sylvia Rimm
ON RAISING KIDS

Sylvia B. Rimm, Ph.D.

Illustrated by
Katherine Raue Maas

Apple Publishing Company
W6050 Apple Road
Watertown, WI 53098-3937

Library of Congress Cataloging in Publication Data

Rimm, Sylvia B.
Sylvia Rimm On Raising Kids

      Bibliography:
      1. Parenting   2. Child Development
      3. Psychology

©1992 by Apple Publishing Company, Subsidiary of
Educational Assessment Service, Inc.
W6050 Apple Road, Watertown, Wisconsin 53098-3937
(800) 475-1118 • FAX (414) 261-6622

Printed and bound in the United States of America.

Second Printing, March, 1994

Illustrations: Katherine Raue Maas

ISBN No. 0-937891-09-6
Library of Congress Catalog Card No. 92-70049

This book is dedicated to my cohost

Tom Clark

in appreciation for his introducing me to my
radio opportunities for helping families.
Tom has always added immensely to the
fun of answering parents' questions.

ACKNOWLEDGMENTS

I would like to thank my staff, Joanne Riedl, Marilyn Knackert, and Barbara Ruder, for their dedicated and careful review of my book and for their excellent feedback. Also, I want to extend my appreciation to the many families who have written and called in the countless questions about raising their kids, which make up the content of my book. Again, I wish to thank my family members who have always provided the underlying inspiration for all my contributions.

TABLE OF CONTENTS

PREFACE

How many times have we all heard people say that parenting is the hardest job in the world although we come to parenting with no real preparation? Even if we have studied child development, taken parenting classes, and read child-rearing books, the information is often contradictory and confusing. When it comes to the everyday questions of raising kids, there simply are no easy answers forthcoming.

Other generations have asked their own parents, and even their grandparents, for help. For this generation, the answers of other generations often don't fit very well. Child-rearing environments have changed drastically. The roles of mothers and fathers are no longer so clearly defined. There are now many more caretakers involved with children. Divorce and single parenting have complicated parenting for many. The media, especially television, plays an important influential role for our youth. I think it's very hard to raise children today.

Parents often feel powerless in guiding their children in a society where there are so many other powerful influences. They search for help for the daily problems which may cause them to feel isolated and lonely. When parents, especially mothers, had more time to provide each other with support, they would often answer each other's questions or at least recognize that they were not alone with their problems on raising kids. In this generation, most families are on "overload." That leaves little time for the encouragement each of us needs when accomplishing the challenging tasks of parenting.

It has been my privilege to answer parents' questions in my Clinic, on radio, on television, in newspapers, by letters, at lectures, and in discussion groups. My answers have been welcomed by parents because they are practical, commonsense, and doable. They are based on solid values that many parents search for in a world invaded by shoddy standards.

Before you read this question-and-answer book, you may want to know the principles which I emphasize. Independence, kindness, love of learning, creative thinking, self-discipline, limit setting, physical and mental fitness, and nonadultizement of the child are central themes I use in guiding parents. My goals always include trying to keep families and schools working together, parents cooperating with each other (whether married or divorced), and consistency among caretakers. I believe that school learning and academic challenge should be clear first priorities because I see achievement as the pathway to building self-confidence in children. However, I view achievement and excellence as including coping with competition and failure, as well as experiencing the pleasure of learning for its own sake.

I believe you may gain much as you read my answers to the questions parents have asked. The questions in my book have come from public radio listeners, letters, and parents in my many audiences. Surely some of their questions will touch your concerns. Many, many parents have assured me I've been helpful to them, so perhaps that will give you the confidence that my answers can be useful to you as well.

If my book is helpful to you, please ask more questions by calling me on my program, *Sylvia Rimm On Raising Kids*, on public radio or by sending me a letter, which I may answer on the air or in newspapers or magazines. Parenting is the most challenging and, hopefully for you, the most wonderful job in the world.

I. PRESCHOOL & PRIMARY

School and Learning

Reading Readiness
of First Grader

Dear Dr. Sylvia,

How do you know when a first grader is learning to read if he really isn't ready or if he isn't trying hard enough? Our son doesn't seem to want to read.

Mother Who is Afraid to Pressure

Dear Mother,

It is usually safe to assume that most first graders are ready to learn to read, but it sounds as if your son is avoiding learning. If it appears that he isn't trying, there's a good chance that he may be lacking in self-confidence or is feeling anxious. Here's some help for relieving the anxiety and encouraging his motivation to read:

1. Don't force him to read aloud to you. All parents feel anxiety if their children are struggling with reading. That anxiety conveys itself to your son, and he will in turn feel worried and unsure of himself. On the other hand, if he really wants to read aloud to you, be sure to find a little time each day to listen and try to enjoy.

2. Continue to read to him. You can read to your family for fun as long as your children are interested. Listening to stories encourages a love of books without any sense of pressure.

3. Let him stay up one half hour later at bedtime provided he'd like to read or look at books in bed. Gradually, children acquire the good habit of reading to themselves and loving books.

4. Encourage him to listen to tapes of books while looking at the pictures. Gradually, he'll automatically associate words. The more he repeats a book, the better. Even spontaneous memorization of the story helps.

5. If you have little preschoolers at home, encourage your son to read to them and to tell them stories. If you have none at home, perhaps the neighbor's children will enjoy his stories. It is wonderful for his confidence and for his love of books. The younger children are not likely to notice his mistakes.

6. Turn the television off for some time each evening. If your son sees you and your husband reading, he'll soon join in the fun.

Not all children learn to read at the same time or as easily. If you follow my suggestions for making reading feel safe, I expect it won't be long before your son becomes more enthusiastic about effort. If you don't see progress in the next few months, ask your school to do an evaluation to determine if there are more extensive problems.

****

Stress on Toddler in Nursery School

Dear Dr. Sylvia,

My son, Scott, is three years old. He started going to day care for the first time. He seemed to be adjusting really well at first. Then we started getting notes from his teacher that he was having problems. A few days later, there was a problem with Scott wetting his pants or getting to the toilet but wetting on the floor. Before this, Scott never had any of these problems at home. Now we are receiving letters stating he needs to work on his motor skills and that he's to be careful when he colors, and that I need to teach him how to scribble and how to hold the crayon correctly. To me this all seems to be too much pressure on Scott. I'm afraid he's getting to feel insecure about all this. If the teacher puts stress on him

in day care and he comes home and I continue to put stress on him some more, how good can this be for him? I just wanted him to go somewhere and enjoy interacting with other children his age. Do you have any advice on this for me?

Stressed Mom

Dear Stressed Mom,

It does indeed seem that your son is showing symptoms of stress. You mentioned his wetting his pants, but you didn't say whether he seems happy to go to day care or is happily playing when you pick him up. Sometimes children show symptoms of stress when they first adjust to a new environment, but the symptoms go away after a few weeks.

The activities of a three-year-old day-care program usually include group play, singing, listening to stories, and small muscle coordination tasks such as working with crayons (mainly scribbling) or painting on an easel. Social skills, such as taking turns and sharing, are typically very important. It should not put pressure on your son if you encourage him to draw or scribble with "fat" crayons. He can even tell you little stories about his pictures, but I promise you that Scott's scribbles are not likely to look very much like artwork.

I would suggest that you ask his teacher if you may observe your son in day care. You'll be able to readily see if he fits in well with the other children. You might also want to see if he is in a mixed-age class and if your son is expected to keep up with four- and five-year-olds. If it is a good day-care center, that's unlikely. You will want to notice if the teachers are patient and calm with the children. You may feel reassured after watching him with other children.

If you feel less anxious, Scott may also feel better and, after a few weeks, may adjust quite nicely. However, if your observation of the school suggests that it sets too high expectations for your son, take him out and either look for a less pressured nursery school or consider forming a play group with a few friends who have children of similar age. You and your friends can rotate providing leadership and teaching the children to play together. However, you too will probably want to include in your activities simple tasks to develop small muscle coordination including "scribbling" pretty pictures.

****

Child Acts Silly During Preschool Work with Parents

Dear Dr. Sylvia,

My question is about our five-year-old son. He's going into kindergarten this fall, and when my wife and I work with him at home with numbers or letters, he starts to laugh and giggle and just lose control. He'll think it's all kind of a joke and just funny stuff. What should we do about that? He won't do that in preschool or with other people, but he'll just start giggling when we work with him.

Impatient Dad

Dear Impatient Dad,

It is good for you and your wife to do a little work with your five-year-old since he'll soon be entering kindergarten. It is also a good sign that he doesn't respond with silliness in preschool. His silly response to you and his mother may be related to anxiety he feels when he works with you.

Plan a regular work time with him for a very short time, less than five minutes at first. Be sure only one adult is with him in the room. Begin with number or letter games first, follow the dots, and coloring or cut and paste until he feels more comfortable with his work time. Rhymes and poems also make learning more interesting. Praise him for being a hard worker during the very first minute and remember, keep the lessons very brief. When you're finished, tell your spouse, within your son's hearing, that he seems to be learning well (referential praise). Be very sure not to do too much at once or expect him to learn too quickly. Stop working before he's ready to stop. When he asks for more, tell him he must wait until the next day because you are too busy. As he asks for more, extend the time very gradually. Soon he'll be begging you for more of your precious time and valuing the time you're willing to spend with him.

Children are very sensitive to anxiety that you feel in teaching them, and your son may feel your teaching as pressure. He may be afraid he can't please you. Shortening the time and selecting fun activities will be likely to have the effect of lifting the pressure.

If that approach doesn't work, skip a few weeks of work time. Continue reading and playing with him. Try again after a few more weeks. Your son's small muscle coordination may be a bit delayed, which seems to happen with many children, but more with boys than girls. Give him a little more time to get ready. When he's feeling ready, he'll stop the silliness and begin enjoying the learning process.

****

Encouraging Child to Sit Still in Kindergarten

Dear Dr. Sylvia,

What suggestions do you have for getting a five-year-old boy to sit still in kindergarten and stay on task?

Restless Dad of Restless Son

Dear Restless Dad,

At least you appreciate your son's difficulty. There are many high-energy persons who have difficulty sitting still, and it is not unusual for me to meet a parent who admits to having the same problem as his/her son or daughter. I'm sure by adulthood, you have discovered some significant solutions for your restlessness and that you also appreciate the requirement for sitting reasonably still in kindergarten.

Actually, I have three relatively easy solutions, one of which will surely be effective. Try only one at a time since if the first works, there is no reason to try either of the other two.

Solution #1:

Have a man-to-boy private talk with your son. Explain that he is growing up, and now that he's in kindergarten, you expect him to sit very still in class and do all his work before he leaves his chair. Tell him that you will ask him each night how well he's doing, and after a few weeks, you expect to contact his teacher to ask her if he's improved. Be very serious during the conversation and leave him with the message that you're counting on him to accomplish this hard job. Pat him on the back or give him a hug. Then check with him privately on his daily progress. Praise him if he thinks he's doing better; encourage him if he says he's having problems. After two weeks, ask his teacher about his progress. Expect improvement.

Solution #2:

This is a teacher solution and can be used with Solution #1 if it doesn't work after about two weeks. Confer with your son's teacher and ask her to read my suggestions or send them in a note to her.

The teacher should take your son aside privately and tell him that she realizes how hard it is for him to sit still, but that kindergartners must be still to do all their work. She should explain that she will be watching to see how hard he's trying, and that if he looks up at her once in awhile, she'll touch her ear as a signal to let him know she sees him trying hard. Solution #2 is almost always effective since it gives private, positive attention to your son's efforts.

Solution #3:

Add Solution #3 to Solutions 1 and 2 only if the others have not been completely effective. This solution is a parent-teacher cooperative effort.

The teacher explains to your son that she will divide the session into two or four parts (depending on whether it is half-day or full-day kindergarten). For each part of the day that he stays in his seat, she will make a star or smiley face on a note which he may take home to you. If he brings his note back with all stars or smiley faces, you can let him choose the dessert for the day or he can play a special game with you. If stars or smiley faces aren't there, express your disappointment but say that you hope he'll try harder the next day. For some high-energy children, sitting still is difficult to accomplish. However, although it may take them some time to actually earn the smiley faces, their concentration and accomplishments almost always improve during the process.

Although your question is about your kindergarten boy, these solutions will work for children from preschool through approximately third grade. If students have at least one leg on their seats, we count that as sufficient sitting still to do their work. However, if they're up and down and all around the room and talking to their friends, little is accomplished. Teaching children "in-seat" behaviors is often simpler than it may appear and is highly effective for early achievement in school.

****

Do Younger Children Learn Faster?

Dear Dr. Sylvia,

I have started teaching kindergarten children math the last three years. I have found that the kindergarten children and first graders can learn number facts faster than the third- and fourth-grade children if they are taught well. I would like to know if it is just because they are very interested or if they can learn easier at that age.

Teaching Nun

Dear Sister,

Your experience is a good one that is surely worth researching. We do know that parents often teach their children math facts in preschool years and that children seem to learn them easily. We also know that children learn music (violin and piano) very easily and differently when they are very young by the Suzuki method. Also, there has been documentation of how easily young children can learn multiple languages. It may be that math, too, can be learned more easily in kindergarten than in third or fourth grade. Although they may only be learning facts by rote and not truly understanding the in-depth processes, learning facts early may make them more confident and efficient math students in later years.

Parents may wish to try teaching children facts at home as well, but they would want to be very careful not to rush or pressure these young children. The traditional card game, War, is a very good one to use for teaching children about numbers under fun and game conditions, and preschool children often learn it (and the numbers on the cards) easily.

Thanks for letting me know about your good work. You may want to apply for a grant to expand and research your project. This nation is very concerned about its children's lack of math skills. The timing is right. Mathematics has always been important, but our government's present concern about it makes it a good time for innovative teaching and research.

****

Too Much Competition for First-Grade Daughter

Dear Dr. Sylvia,

Is there an age level that would be "too early" for competition? For example, my first-grade daughter breaks down crying when she can't spell a word in her class spelling contest and she wants to drop out. Should I ask her teacher not to make her compete? I'm afraid she won't want to go to school.

Anxious Mom

Dear Anxious Mom,

It is hard to watch little first graders experience failures, but it is not too early for them to gradually learn some important competition lessons like 1) no one wins all the time, 2) it's all right to make a mistake, and 3) you can improve if you practice.

Spelling bees are a moderate form of competition that have been around for a long time. Give her practice words for ten minutes a day and help her chart the number of words she spells correctly. She'll be able to see her own improvement on her chart and will feel less anxious about participating in school.

Most important, don't give her too much sympathy or conversation for her tears. Instead, joke about them or just explain that she needs to learn to be a better sport. Teach her competition by playing board games with her, but be sure not to let her win all the time.

First grade is definitely not too early to learn about competition. If you accept her tears casually and realistically, she will become much less anxious and will even become a good speller.

****

Holding Back Bright Preschooler

Dear Dr. Sylvia,

Our daughter is a very young kindergartner and her teacher has suggested that she is immature and should be held out a year so that she will fit in better. However, she has been reading since she was four and can count to 100 and do simple addition and subtraction. We worry that holding her back will cause her boredom in later years, but we don't want her to feel too pressured either.

Puzzled Parents

Dear Puzzled Parents,

You have good reason to be puzzled and concerned. Your first step is to request an evaluation by your school psychologist or a local private psychologist who specializes in evaluating gifted children. Step two is to ask the teacher to describe your daughter's immature behaviors.

If your child tests in the very superior IQ range, she may be better off being young in the class. Research in the field of gifted children continuously finds that children who are accelerated or entered early usually do better with the additional challenge.

Girls tend to mature earlier than boys. Sometimes symptoms of immaturity are indicative that a child has not been given enough independence. These same symptoms may also mean a child has been given too much power. You would be able to know that better after the

teacher describes the problems. Two of my books that will help you to correct the problems are *How To Parent So Children Will Learn* and *Underachievement Syndrome: Causes and Cures.*

Gifted children often adjust better to older children than children of the same age. The test results and parent and teacher observations of the child's adjustment for three or four months will help you to make better decisions for her future.

****

Family Relationships and Discipline

Daughter Won't Take "No" for Answer

Dear Dr. Sylvia,

How can I handle my preschool daughter who won't take "no" for an answer?

Defeated Mom

Dear Defeated Mom,

The years ahead will be much worse if you feel defeated now. All children must learn to accept "no" sometimes, and children should never receive constant "noes" from their parents.

Since your child is quite young, diversion is an easy first tool. Small children can be easily distracted. As you say "no" to the activity your child is presently involved in, distract her with another activity. Distraction is actually effective much of the time.

If distraction doesn't work, pick her up and put her in her crib or bed to play. Gates work well for keeping small children in their rooms. If she cries, don't discuss or argue with her. After she settles down, ask if she's ready to come out. She will have certainly forgotten about her negative activity at this point and will be her happy self again. Sometimes children actually prefer staying in their rooms to play after their time-out is over, and that's all right too.

Childproof your house to a reasonable extent by putting your special possessions on high shelves. After the playpen stage is over, use gates to contain children within a room or two. Rotate toys for them occasionally so that they have variety. All of this will prevent you from saying "no" continuously. Too many parent "noes" dampen children's initiative.

However, when you do say "no," be firm. Don't let kids argue or temper-tantrum you into getting their way. It's tempting for parents to want to say "yes" to their children because they think their children will like them better. Sometimes parents say "yes" only because their children have worn them down. Parents who don't set limits for children are eventually viewed as "wimps " by their kids and are hardly ever respected. Children need parents who are kind, but who are also *in charge*. Study after study shows that children do better in authoritative families. Either too permissive or authoritarian (both extremes) parents seem to cause problems for their children. Your daughter needs to learn to accept "no" now, but remember to avoid giving her too many "noes."

****

Using Time-Out Effectively

Dear Dr. Sylvia,

Can you explain how to effectively use a "time-out?" At what age does a child understand time-out?

Tired of Screaming

Dear Tired of Screaming,

Time-out is extremely effective with children beginning at about age two; however, it is done quite differently for toddlers than it is for preschoolers, and differently still for school-age children.

For toddlers, explaining briefly and distracting them to other activities can be your first discipline approach. However, temper tantrums and angry crying to get one's way can be timed-out in crib, bed, or gated room. A few minutes of time-out after the child has quieted down is usually enough to teach the child that his/her naughty behavior will not be accepted. If you can manage to time-out before you lose your temper, it makes the time-out more effective since the child has more confidence in your consistency. Sometimes toddlers fall asleep when they've been timed-out. Let them nap. Their acting out may have been exacerbated by their exhaustion.

For preschool children and school-age children who are reasonably compliant, if they've misbehaved or have had a tantrum, they may willingly go to their room when sent. Five to ten minutes of quiet time are usually enough to settle them down. If they slam the door behind themselves, don't respond, and they will typically stop slamming. If you angrily remind them not to slam the door, it will probably go on for as long as you keep reminding them.

For the strong-willed and too-powerful child, the rule for an effective time-out from my book *How to Parent So Children Will Learn* follows:

RECIPE FOR SUCCESSFUL TIME-OUTS (FOLLOW EXACTLY)

1. All adults and older siblings must follow the same rules.

2. One adult tells the child briefly (two sentences or less) that the consequence for specific enumerated naughty behaviors will be to stay in his/her room for ten minutes of quiet with the door closed.

3. The naughty behaviors should be specified. Don't select all, just the worst (e.g., hitting, temper tantrums, talking back to parents).

4. If the child is likely to open the door when it's closed, arrange it so the door can be locked from the outside. Door handles may be reversed or a latch can be used. One parent

suggested looping a rope from one door handle to another door handle. For most very powerful children, some kind of lock is required, at least initially.

5. For the first and every time the child misbehaves in the stated way, the child should be escorted to the room without the parent losing his/her temper and without giving any further explanation beyond one sentence.

6. If the child slams the door, loses his or her temper, bangs on walls, throws toys, screams, shouts, or talks, there is should be absolutely no response from anyone. Expect the first few times to be terrible. Remember, absolutely **NO** response from anyone.

7. Set the timer *only* when the child is quiet (not screaming, tantruming, or using disrespectful language).

8. After ten minutes, open the door to permit the child to leave. There should be no further explanation or apology or warning or discussion of love. Act as if nothing unusual has happened. **DON'T HUG!**

9. Repeat as necessary.

10. After a week or two, only a warning of the closed door should be necessary to prevent the undesirable behavior.

11. You may use "time-out" for warning purposes. Give only one warning. **ALWAYS** follow through.

12. Your child will become calmer, appear more secure, and be much better behaved.

The typical mistakes parents make are listed here:

1. They permit children to time themselves out, in which case they will often slam the door. Parents respond by telling them not to slam the door. In that way, children recognize that they're powerful, more powerful than parents, and they continue to slam the door.

2. Sometimes parents will make the mistake of talking to children when they call out and ask how much more time they have. Parents may actually start arguing with them. The conversation cancels the effect of withdrawn attention.

3. Some parents are hesitant about locking the door and will stand holding the door closed. The child knows that the parent is holding the door; thus, the power struggle continues.

4. Sometimes after children have thrown things around their room, parents insist that they go back to pick up what they have thrown around. Another power struggle ensues in which case children are in charge of the parent by argument again.

5. Sometimes parents use time-out only after they've yelled and screamed and lost their temper. That isn't effective. It should be executed calmly, as if parents are in charge.

The purpose of time-out is not punishment, but only calm limit setting and teaching your child reasonable self-control. Once you learn to use it effectively with your child, it won't require frequent use. A warning will usually be enough because your child will learn that you mean what you say.

Many parents have told me they worry that their children will learn to hate their rooms. Although I've suggested time-out for literally thousands of children, I've never heard of a single child who learned to hate his or her room. Time-out is so much more effective than scolding, losing tempers, spanking, and the many awful things that parents do when children have too much power. Once you learn to use it effectively, I know you'll feel better about your parenting.

****

Time-Out for Toddler

Dear Dr. Sylvia,

I've read your book How To Parent So Children Will Learn and really enjoyed it. My son is 15 months old and he's starting to misbehave. I think he's too young for time-outs. I'm wondering if there is a mini time-out for when he's two, and if I use his crib, would there be any risk of his being afraid of his crib?

Mom, Anxious To Set Limits

Dear Mom,

Even at 15 months of age, toddlers require limits. However, they're a little young to "time-out." Usually distraction to another toy and childproofing his environment take care of most of the limit setting. Distraction is amazingly effective since little guys his age concentrate on one thing at a time, and involvement with a new toy seems to prevent any further naughty activity.

As he gets a little older, a mini time-out may be in order after several unsuccessful distractions or naughty behaviors. Of course, you're right that his crib is an ideal location. Leave a few toys for him to play with. He may cry a little or just play. Sometimes toddlers fall asleep because the "naughtiness" was actually sleepiness. No special timing is required nor is a closed door. Since your little fellow will either be happily playing for awhile or napping, that results in absolutely no crib trauma, although it does set a reasonable limit.

When your little boy moves to a bed in which he might not stay if timed-out, be sure his room is child-safe and put a gate at the door. Stay out of view. Closing the door might be frightening to a two-year-old, and the gate will be sufficent to set an appropriate limit. A two-year-old needs only a few minutes of settling down before he can come out. Incidentally, although we've used time-out for thousands of children, I've never heard of a child being traumatized by the brief time-outs I recommend. They are effective and, when handled calmly, are so much more humane than the confusing anger, warnings, overreasoning, and more anger that are often typical.

****

Uncontrollable Granddaughter

Dear Dr. Sylvia,

My four-year-old granddaughter is often uncontrollable. Everyone who sees her tells us she needs discipline, and although my daughter is trying, she is nearly beside herself in just what to do.

Last time I visited, we had supper together, and we told her she must eat all of her supper to get a piece of pie. She didn't eat all of her supper and later, of course,

she wanted pie. When she was told she couldn't have any because she hadn't eaten her supper, she started crying and screaming. My daughter took her to her room. She cried and screamed and kicked the door. My daughter returned to the room and spanked her. That stopped the kicking, but she continued to scream and cry until she fell asleep.

We don't know what the right thing is to do anymore. We love the child, but she just won't listen. Can you give us some advice?

A Loving Grandma

Dear Loving Grandma,

I feel certain that I can help you, your daughter, and your granddaughter. Begin by putting **very** small portions of food on her plate. Let her know she may ask for more if she'd like. Use the pie in the same reward manner that you have in the past. If she doesn't eat her meal, place it in the refrigerator until pie time. When the pie is served, offer her the choice of eating her remaining cold dinner and pie, or no dinner and no pie.

If she continues to refuse her meal and cries and screams, quietly escort her to her room and explain that she must stay there until she quiets down. Don't call in to her, and definitely, don't spank her. I understand that your daughter doesn't want to abuse her, but it sounds as if she may be losing control. When she's been quiet for five minutes, let her know she may come out. If she asks for her supper, give her the remaining supper, but ***don't reheat it***. If not, forget it. She will surely remember this lesson next time.

It sounds as if your granddaughter has too much power for her four years and is mainly in control of her mother. That may cause many problems in the future.

****

Powerful Nephew

Dear Dr. Sylvia,

I have a question about a 4½-year-old. Actually, he's our nephew. His mom is single, and he seems to be running the household. She can't understand why we don't like to come and visit because everything is centered around this kid. How do we tell her? If he doesn't want to go to bed at bedtime, he puts up such a fit that he doesn't go to bed. He doesn't really sleep in his own bed. He still sleeps with his mom all the time. We don't go around much because he is so intolerable, we can hardly stand to be there. He won't come visit us because when we set the rules at our house, he has to follow them. He doesn't even really like us anymore.

Disappointed Aunt and Uncle

Dear Disappointed Aunt and Uncle,

You are truly important to your sister and especially important to her son. Your observations seem appropriate. No 4½-year-old should be running a household, nor will his kindergarten teacher appreciate his excessive power. It is difficult to tell a single mother, who may indeed view her only child as "royalty," that there are alternative techniques to use. She will probably resent your advice unless she asks for it.

First of all, you might mention that boys who sleep with their mothers often become exceedingly resentful and angry when their mothers choose to begin dating a man. The intense and intimate relationship of sleeping together causes a child to feel very threatened if an adult male should want to take over that bed.

You might also suggest, Uncle, that you would be happy to do some special one-to-one activities with your nephew since you've heard that male role models are important to young boys. Be sure to make these activities separate from his mother and your wife. Enjoy and have fun with your nephew, but look for opportunities to tell him how important it is for him to listen to his mom, to sleep in his own bed, and to be responsible. Let him know that each time you do a fun activity together, you'll ask him if he's been good at home with his mom. Hopefully, this will support your sister and give her a little more power. Your spending a day with your nephew every few weeks will give her some valued free time, and she will appreciate it.

You can really be a very powerful role model for your nephew. Perhaps when you bring him home from a day of fun, your sister will ask about his behavior. When you say it was good, she may even ask how you discipline him. That could give you the opportunity to explain how to be firm and set limits.

I know you'd like to do more, but even these few suggestions can make quite a difference for your nephew. If your nephew's mother doesn't learn to set limits for her son now, by kindergarten the teacher will see the problem and recommend that she get help. My book *How To Parent So Children Will Learn* can guide her in setting limits.

If you're sensitive and subtle in your suggestions, and you do your part to help, eventually your sister will appreciate your effort. I can't promise you she'll thank you, but her son will be the beneficiary of your kindness, and that's the best thanks you can get.

****

Son Doesn't Care
About Punishment

Dear Dr. Sylvia,

My six-year-old son (adopted from Korea) doesn't seem to care when I punish him. He says, "I don't care if you take all my toys away." Also, when I praise him or reassure him, he sounds surprised and seems unsure that I mean it. Nothing seems to work.

Mother of Six-Year-Old

Dear Mother of Six-Year-Old,

It sounds as if you may be in a power struggle with your son and that he may have convinced you that he's won.

First, it's important to realize that when children say they don't care about a punishment, it usually means they *do* care. They tell you they don't care in hopes that they can convince you to take the punishment away. However, the "don't cares" usually frustrate parents so much that parents add further punishments or keep changing them. Your son sounds too powerful. Here are some suggestions:

1. Praise him mildly and casually rather than extremely. The extreme praise may make him feel pressured to live up to the praise. Here are some examples of extreme praise that you should *avoid*:

Your painting is so good it belongs in a museum.

You're the smartest kid in first grade.

I love you more than anyone in the world.

More appropriate praise would include:

You seem to really enjoy painting. Pick out your favorite picture, and we'll hang it on the refrigerator.

You're a really good reader. Tell me about that story.

I love you very much. (If he asks, "More than anyone?" say, "No. I love your dad in a different way and your sister in a different way, but no one more than others.")

Praise statements like you're kind, you're a hard worker, you take good initiative, and I like the way you think are all appropriately encouraging.

2. Punish briefly, consistently, and firmly. Before you hand out a punishment, tell your child you want to think it over. A few minutes of thinking will cool your temper and

keep you more realistic. When you choose a
punishment, try to make it fit the problem.
For example, if your son has broken something he wasn't supposed to touch, calculate
the cost, and let him choose from a couple of
ways to earn the money for replacement.

When you threaten to punish, don't threaten a second
time. Instead, follow through, preferably calmly. That
way your son will know that you mean what you say.
When the punishment is over, don't remind him not to
do it again or say, "I told you so." He'll learn by
experience not to repeat these punished behaviors. Please
don't expect him to admit that your punishment worked.
Hardly any children do.

It would be nice if kids would apologize and
acknowledge to you that they were wrong. Some of the
kids who are most willing to apologize, however, are the
very ones who repeat the problem behavior right after
they've apologized. The apology becomes a manipulative
habit.

Be positive. Don't overpunish, but if you do, stay
with your punishment and ignore your son's I don't cares
except as a tip-off to you that he does care.

****

Sibling Rivalry

Dear Dr. Sylvia,

Mine is a sibling rivalry question. I have an eight-, six-, and four-year-old, but my four-year-old is a little old for her age, and the six-year-old is a little young. It's like having a pair of five-year-olds. They spend every waking minute snipping at each other. They can't be in the same room unless they're actively involved in something. They could be doing two different things, and they'll still be arguing. It's like they're parallel playing, but they're arguing at the same time. It's terrible. Riding in a car is a nightmare. I don't know what to do about this because it gets really annoying. I'm ready to . . . you know . . . it's terrible!

Exasperated Mom

Dear Exasperated Mom,

Let me give you some guidelines that will be really helpful to you and assure you that you will never make sibling rivalry disappear. Sibling rivalry is a natural response for children who are reasonably assertive. The only way you would have sibling rivalry disappear is if one child gave orders and the other took orders, and then, of course, they wouldn't fight. But if they're assertive, they'll have some differences some of the time. The extreme sibling rivalry you described is a little more uncomfortable than the typical sibling rivalry, but you can do some neat things to help with the situation.

First of all, insist on some alone time for both children so that they're not always playing together. If they're always playing together, obviously they're going to argue more, and they really should have some separate time. It's healthy for their independence and imagination.

Second of all, when they have an argument, let them know that you are going to stay out of it within the following limits: If they physically hit each other or if they get too loud so that you can't stand the noise, then you're going to get involved. However, you will *not* mediate. Don't try to determine who was right or wrong. You'll never be able to do that. If they're hitting each other, then ask them to go into two separate rooms for ten minutes. If they're just arguing too loud, ask them to argue in another room so you can't hear the noise.

Remember, don't mediate, because if you mediate, you'll only make the problem worse. Each child tries to get you on his or her side and the rivalry increases. Here are some other suggestions to help with sibling rivalry:

1. A token reward system can be used temporarily to reinforce children's cooperative behavior. That works well particularly when siblings are required to spend a great amount of time together, for example, during summer vacation or a long car ride. By dividing the

day into two or three sections, children can receive a point for each time period of cooperative behavior. Early morning to noon might be one section of the day. Afternoon to dinner or evening meal would be a second section, and the evening meal to bedtime would be a third section. Siblings would only receive a point if both (or all) children are being nice to each other. That encourages their cooperation. The goal is to accumulate a small number (10 to 15 points) toward an activity which the children can participate in, like going out for pizza, going to a movie, or renting a special video. You'll know that your program has been effective when one child hits or teases and the other one says that it's all right because he or she knew it was all in fun.

2. Surprise plannings can be used to build cooperative sibling feelings. When one parent gets the children together to plan a surprise for the other parent or for a third child, then the children get involved in cooperative planning and feel closer. Any alliance with a positive goal builds unity. The secrets of gift giving, surprises, and parties seem to unite brothers and sisters and diminish arguing. Special projects or planning for Grandma,

Grandpa, Aunt, Uncle, a neighbor, or a friend encourages a sense of togetherness that comes from joint efforts. Parents can effectively use cooperative strategies multiple times to build sibling solidarity.

3. Sibling rivalry almost always affects children's achievement. Children tend to easily assume that their achievement appears more impressive if their brothers' and sisters' achievements are not as good. Explain to your children that it's nice to have a "whole smart family" and that achievement by one child doesn't limit achievement by the others. I would suggest that children be encouraged to admit any feelings of jealousy. Most children have them. Teach them to handle these feelings better by accepting the challenge of openly admiring their sisters or brothers. That seems to help everyone and minimizes the put-downs.

4. If your children put each other down, don't take sides at the time. However, you should communicate your concern to the one who is doing the putting down in privacy. There's a much better chance of improved behavior if you don't correct the child in front of siblings.

5. Don't appoint your achiever to the role of tutor for your underachiever. It will serve only as a daily put-down for the other; he or she may not understand or be able to express those feelings. Children often say they appreciate their siblings' help, but they also say it makes them feel "dumb."

Probably what will help you most is knowing that if you refuse to take sides, eventually your children will become closer. By young adulthood, they will have learned that it's possible to share their parents' love and they'll finally truly appreciate their siblings.

Eight-year-old Jean Ann described her new relationship to her big brother this way. "We used to nag at each other all the time, but then Mom separated us every time we'd fight, so we just don't do it as much. It's not fun being separated so much."

****

Sibling Rivalry Between
Close-Age Children

Dear Dr. Sylvia,

In your book, you talk about sibling rivalry among children who are close in age. Our girls are 11 months apart. The older child is bright and competitive. The younger child is full of anger, disappointment, and arguments. They are preschoolers. What can I do to help the younger child develop happiness and self-confidence from this point on?

Torn Mother

Dear Torn Mother,

You will actually find that your daughters' closeness will be a joy as well as a frustration if you can avoid some simple pitfalls. Parents whose children are so close in age often tend to treat them equally and involve them in similar activities because the age difference is so small. Certainly having some activities together is fine and makes it easier when you chauffeur them, but if possible, the girls should have separate rooms, separate clothes, and at least some separate activities. Hopefully they are also in separate preschool classes. Most important, each needs a little individual time with you and with their dad to minimize their competitive feelings.

Since they are close in age, they will probably play together much of the time and be good company for each other. However, some of the time, permit each to invite her own friend over and encourage them to play separately. Perhaps one can have a friend at your home while the other goes to a friend's home. The younger one should have some opportunity to play with younger or less dominant children so she has some leadership experiences, and the older one should have the chance to be with friends who may not always take orders from her.

Try not to get into the habit of either rescuing your younger daughter when she pouts or becoming too negative with her. It will only make her become more set in her negative habits.

Most important, when you talk about your younger daughter to other adults, e.g., friends and relatives within her hearing (referential speaking), please don't emphasize or even mention her negative attitude. The more she hears about her problems, the less she will feel she can do anything to change them. Instead, comment on her nice smile, her kindness, or her initiative, both directly to her and to other adults within her hearing.

It sounds as if your little girl has a difficult act to follow in her older sister. You'll need to find her some places out of her sister's shadow so you and she can discover the wonderful light within her. Since your girls are only preschoolers, you can feel optimistic about changing this negative pattern and helping both daughters to be positive and confident.

****

Social and Emotional Concerns

Building Self-Confidence in Small Children

Dear Dr. Sylvia,

I have two small children (six and two years old) and would like to know the best way to build self-confidence in them. Isn't self-confidence one of the best tools parents can give their children?

Mom

Dear Mom,

You're right. Self-confidence is crucial for children. It permits them to feel good about themselves and is basic to their achievement as well as to forming good relationships. However, self-confidence, like happiness, is an elusive concept. In a sense, some of us keep earning our self-confidence throughout life and never quite arrive, while others seem to have so much confidence that it gets them into trouble (they may lack humility).

Realistic self-confidence appears to grow best from a three-pronged foundation. The first is obvious. All children need to feel loved by important others. I'm sure you love your children or you wouldn't be asking about confidence. Be sure to express your love to them with both words and hugs. However, don't mix your love messages with punishment. Children become confused.

The other two foundational stones are more difficult to teach: responsibility and respect for limits. Responsibility teaches children that they are competent. As they learn they can carry through on home chores, academic tasks, social activities, and communication skills, they develop a sense of accomplishment which gives them the experience and courage to risk further academic and socially appropriate adventures. Love alone cannot replace the solid experiences of successes and failures that gradually permit children to earn competence and confidence.

Teaching children to respect limits prevents them from feeling overconfident. Limits encourage sensitivity to others' needs and respect for the interests, talents, and abilities of their friends and family members. Limit setting prevents children from being pushy, aggressive, disrespectful, and continuously argumentative. Parents who have difficulty setting limits for children will soon find life at home quite unpleasant. Children who have not learned to respect limits often believe they have more wisdom than their parents. While they appear self-confident and even bossy, their adolescence and your adulthood is often one of major mood swings since their confidence is tied to domination without limits. When persons in their lives refuse to be dominated by them, they are likely to feel depressed and angry.

While the foundations of healthy confidence are clear, parents are not the only persons involved in the process.

Peers, teachers, siblings, and other important adults contribute to your children's confidence. As parents, we can't control everything in our children's lives, but we can guide our children toward having good school and friendship experiences. This isn't a step-by-step recipe for building your children's confidence, but hopefully your sensitivity to the importance of teaching responsibility and limits will encourage you to not make your children's world so easy for them that you prevent them from feeling good about themselves. Specific suggestions for teaching responsibility and setting limits are included in my book *How To Parent So Children Will Learn.*

****

Girl Insists on Being Fictional Characters

Dear Dr. Sylvia:

My four-year-old daughter is gifted, exuberant, funny, strong-willed, and tough-minded. She has assumed the identity of fictional characters since she was two years old, going through Maria (Sound of Music), Pinocchio, Cinderella, Charlotte, and Dorothy (Oz). She usually insists on being called by the character of the month and often acts the stories out. Her current person is Carly, her best friend who is eight. A real person is more complicated. She even insisted on being called Carly

when she went back to preschool. She can be very stubborn and demanding about it. Except for occasional tantrums, she is well-adjusted. She is an only child, and we are professionals in our forties, happily married.

Is this going too far? Should we insist on her being called by her real name? I am a psychologist, and this has my colleagues and me baffled! Thanks.

Baffled Mom

Dear Baffled Psychologist Mom,

I always feel a bit awed and flattered when I'm questioned by another psychologist, but I'm pleased to answer your question and hope that you will consider my answer seriously.

Your daughter sounds like a delightful, imaginative child. Creative persons often have had a history of childhood imaginary friends. However, as an only child, there is a great risk of your child becoming "attention addicted" and too powerful. Attention-addicted children frequently feel attention deprived when they enter school where they must share attention with 25 other children. "Too powerful" children learn to assume that they should only do what they want to do and get angry when they are required to comply with parents, teachers, or friends. If at age four you say your daughter is sometimes "very stubborn and demanding," imagine how those difficult characteristics may worsen by adolescence. You may lose the opportunity to guide her.

Explain to your daughter that you thoroughly enjoy her imaginary play and will be happy to watch her put on her plays for a little time each day. However, also explain that when her pretend play is over, you will again call her by her real name. In preschool, she should expect the same approach. During playtime, she may play pretend, and her playmates may call her Carly or Cinderella or Maria. However, her teachers and friends will call her by her real name when the play is over.

It is actually very important that imaginative children learn to differentiate pretend from real. If they don't, the pretend begins to invade their real lives. They easily extend stories, fabricate, and lie so comfortably and convincingly that it becomes difficult for parents to know when to believe them. Sometimes even the children become confused. While this kind of dishonesty is not intentional and not the same as adult lying, it can easily lead to serious adult problems.

Help your daughter feel secure in her creative play by setting limits for her imagination and by teaching her to clearly identify what is real and what is imaginary. Most of all, enjoy her delightful imagination and encourage her to continue the fun within your safe limits.

****

Child Has Fear of Fire;
Won't Sleep Alone

Dear Dr. Sylvia,

I wonder if schools may be teaching our children to be too fearful. After Fire Prevention Week, my six-year-old daughter dreamed that our house was burning down and now refuses to go to bed without me lying at her side. If I try to leave her, she cries and trembles in hysterical tears and I feel I should stay with her. I've already explained how rarely fires occur and that we've taken all safety precautions. I'm not sure if she really is afraid or just likes me lying at her side.

Anxious Mom

Dear Anxious Mom,

It is really true that children must learn techniques to save themselves in an emergency fire and that these techniques may cause them some temporary fears. However, your anxiety about the issue and your sleeping with your daughter nightly are probably prolonging the agony. Your first response was correct.

You explained to your daughter the unlikeliness of the risk but the importance of knowing how she should respond. However, once is enough. Continued explanations will only make her more anxious. Now explain once that you have other work to do and can no longer lie at her side when she goes to sleep.

Hug her and tuck her in with her favorite stuffed animals and permit her to leave her bedroom light on as long as she would like. You may or may not turn it off when she falls asleep, depending on her choice. If she refuses to stay in bed, insist. Explain that you will close the door unless she stays in bed, but will be happy to leave it open otherwise.

Light and an open door will probably be enough to permit her to sleep independently. Walk away calmly and prepare yourself to hear some anxious tears on her first night alone. Absolutely *don't* go back to sleeping with her or reassuring her. After one or two nights, the tears will disappear, and after a few more nights, the fears will diminish or disappear too. Fortunately, lights feel very protective.

****

Dealing With People Who Call Son "Shy"

Dear Dr. Sylvia,

My son is going to be four years old, and he is very shy. My wife and I don't try to reinforce this, but other well-meaning people will; for example, if we meet a neighbor, or a friend comes over, he'll hide behind our legs, and they'll say, "Oh, he's shy." Now, it's gotten to the point where he runs around the house saying, "I'm very shy, I'm very shy." What's an appropriate response for me to make when another person says in front of him that he's shy, and is there anything else that I can do to help him?

Perceptive Dad

Dear Perceptive Dad,

I'm glad that you and your wife are avoiding calling your son shy, because that is a very common mistake that parents make about shy children. The term I use when adults talk to each other about a child as if the child isn't present is "referential speaking." Referential speaking is very powerful since children assume that if adults are saying something to each other, it is surely true. They often accept it as a label and may even assume that since they are biologically shy, they can't change.

You can use referential speaking as a positive technique for your shy son. Say to your wife when your four-year-old is within hearing, "Did you notice how friendly Jason is becoming? He doesn't seem to be as shy as he used to be?" This will reinforce his social behavior and help him change his self-image.

As to other people's comments about your son's shyness, you could point out to these people that he seems to be outgrowing his shyness, or if it's relatives,

you could talk to them confidentially and share the following tips that come from my book *How To Parent So Children Will Learn.*

Referential speaking is conversation between adults about children within the hearing of those children. It has potential for significant positive or negative impact on children.

1. Negative examples include:

   a. References to a child's shyness, disorganization, sloppiness, slow speed, etc. These feel like labels to children and take away their power to improve.

   b. Comments about how "impossible" the child is emphasize parent power-lessness and children's powerfulness. They foster children's disrespect for their parents.

2. Adults' descriptions of positive behaviors, such as kindness, consideration, hard work, independence, effort, and perseverance, are likely to encourage children to continue such favorable behaviors.

3. Positive descriptions which are exaggerated, such as brilliant, best, most beautiful, extraordinary, and perfect, serve to please children temporarily but eventually cause them to feel extreme pressure when they try to live up to these impossible compliments.

****

Encouraging Shy Children

Dear Dr. Sylvia,

With a shy child, don't you feel you sometimes have to push them into social situations, etc., to make them try different activities?

Husband of Overprotective Wife

Dear Husband,

Shy children often need to be supported, encouraged, and, yes, even forced to become involved in activities. However, select the important activities and then be matter-of-fact and firm. You may even permit them to choose any of two or three activities, but do insist on their making some choice. Avoid power struggles. Don't get in a pattern of saying they should become involved and then permitting them to persuade you to change your decision.

Avoid calling them shy or referring to them as shy when you talk to other adults. It makes them feel powerless about changing their shy behavior. Instead, assume they will participate and stay positive. Shy behaviors are probably partly inherited and partly learned. Even biologically shy children can learn appropriate social involvement and usually do if parents don't overprotect or shelter them too much. However, don't insist on so much involvement that your children feel constantly pushed. Too much pressure may cause them to retreat further. If parents can avoid either sheltering too much or pushing too much (both extremes), shy children will learn to participate in a variety of activities, and they will become more comfortable in most social environments.

****

Youngest Child in Family Afraid to Take Risks

Dear Dr. Sylvia,

What should I do with my youngest child who's afraid to try things because he may not do as well as his older siblings?

Mother of Three

Dear Mother of Three,

Youngest children are not known for their risk taking and feel particular pressure when their older siblings are highly successful. That isn't a pressure parents put on their child, but one that may come automatically with "younger child" territory.

Here are a few tips to help you. First, be sure *not* to treat your children equally. There should be clear age-status markers of privilege and responsibility that children reach as they grow older. For example, older children should be allowed later bedtime, receive more allowance, and have more complex chore responsibilities than younger children. Younger children will then recognize that there are age markers that they'll eventually attain.

Second, be sure not to overprotect that youngest child. When sibling rivalry sets in, as it always does, don't mediate the battles to protect the "baby," or that's what he or she becomes. The younger one often traps the older one into arguments to gain Mother's protection.

Third, encourage the youngest child to enter some activities that the older children were not involved in so they can have the exploring opportunities that your older children were afforded. That shouldn't mean that they can't select activities selected by their siblings, but only that they are not restricted to the same activities. Scholarship is an exception. Expect them all to take school seriously and point out to the younger children how nice it is to have a "whole smart family" reputation in the schools. Explain that the family reputation for being a good student depends on a good attitude about learning, interest, and consistent effort.

Fourth, don't let youngest children "out of" responsibilities because you're too tired to teach a third child how to do the task, and it's easier to have the older children do it.

Fifth, don't call him or her the "baby" of the family. That's tempting, but it slows their growing up.

Sixth, do encourage their leadership opportunities with younger children in the neighborhood or younger cousins or relatives.

Seventh, and very important, be sure not to confide in them about your worries about their older siblings or the naughty things older siblings may be doing. Their temptation will be to try to stay in that tight intimacy with you by avoiding any pitfalls in order to be the "good" kid. The price they will pay is learning to avoid risk for fear they might not be good or entirely successful.

Younger children can grow up to be responsible, achieving, and even leading adults. That happens more easily if parents help them to see there is privilege and responsibility that comes with time and if they avoid overprotecting them. Please remember, don't call him or her "baby." That's a hard label to outgrow.

****

Instilling Self-Esteem
Without Overpraising

Dear Dr. Sylvia,

I have two children. The oldest is almost 2½. I really feel that instilling self-esteem is so important for them, and I don't know how to do it without overpraising them. I've heard conflicting advice about telling them how well they're doing as they accomplish things on their own, but at the same time, I'm afraid that my daughter in particular seems to do things in order to receive our praise instead of doing things for herself.

Mother Who's Puzzled About
Too Much Praise

Dear Mom Who's Puzzled About Overpraise,

When I write or talk about overpraise, I worry that moms and dads will take my advice too literally and will think that it's wrong to praise children or harmful for children to want to do things to get their attention. A positive environment in which children learn and grow almost always includes enthusiastic praise. A little "overpraise" is unlikely to harm children, and no praise will certainly cause problems. It's normal and healthy for preschool children to want to please their parents and other adults. However, parents also should be teaching children to persevere, sustain interest, and derive intrinsic pleasure from their activities.

If you keep in mind that praise is a way of communicating your values to your children, and your words are their guide to eventually setting goals for themselves, you can develop a better sense of what praise words are appropriate. If the typical words you use are too extreme, they will assume that their parents expect those accomplishments from them. Here are some examples of appropriate praise words for children:

You're a good thinker.

You don't quit.

That's a good idea.

You're very inventive.

You really persevere.

You look really nice.

You're so independent.

You really love to learn.

You're so interested in animals (or another topic).

Now here are some overpraise statements that might cause children to feel pressured:

You're perfect.

You look absolutely gorgeous.

That was a brilliant idea.

I bet you're the smartest child in your class.

You paint like Picasso.

You're the greatest.

You're our king (queen).

Even those high-praise statements do no harm if they are infrequent. Sometimes grandparents or neighbors are the culprits, so you may want to gently ask them to be a bit more moderate in their praise.

If you are worried that your little girl is attention addicted and wants your praise too frequently, then you can easily guide her gradually toward somewhat less frequent praise. For example, if your daughter wants admiration for every picture she draws, you could suggest that she draw a whole group of pictures and bring you her favorite when she's done. By moving your praises to her increased time on task, she will automatically learn to enjoy her process more and become better at being less dependent on attention.

Please remember that praise is really important and healthy for children. Certainly children thrive in a positive and enthusiastic environment. Actually, if you have more than one child around your home, there is little risk. The first child or an "only" child is most at risk of overpraise and attention addiction.

****

Problem With Neighbor Girl

Dear Dr. Sylvia,

My three-year-old daughter has a little playmate who's also three and lives next door. Every time they get together, they seem to fight. I think the problem is with the other little girl. When my daughter plays with other children, she doesn't seem to fight with them or get quite as angry. She gets really frustrated. It's almost impossible for me to separate the two because they live right next door to each other. I find myself getting frustrated, and I just don't know what to do about this. Do you think this is just something that they'll eventually outgrow?

Mom Who Can't Move

Dear Mom Who Won't Have To Move,

It's time to talk to the girl's mother about the problem, but please do it carefully. Don't tell her that your daughter rarely gets angry at other children. Instead, just suggest that you set up some simple play rules for the girls. If they're playing at either home and they are not happy with each other, they can be sent home for the remainder of the day. If one of you is babysitting for the other, get permission to separate the girls for a little while until they are calm again. Also, you and your neighbor should decide on some family time where the girls are not together so that they don't become dependent on each other and can each have some uninterrupted privacy.

Now observe your three-year-old as she plays with your neighbor's daughter. They may need to learn some simple social skills, like how to take turns and how to share. They may even require some of your direction for their activities and some suggestions about what are appropriate or inappropriate behaviors. Be careful that you are not biased toward your own daughter and be fair to the little neighbor girl. Mothers of preschoolers must typically do much teaching of social behaviors.

If your daughter seems to do better with other children than with her neighbor, it may only be that she sees this friend much more frequently, or it may be that they are not suited to one another. If you make some effort to improve the girls' interactions and your efforts are not very effective, limiting their time together seems the only reasonable alternative. That may be difficult at first, but once you change the frequency of the relationship, the children will learn to accept your limits. They may truly appreciate each other a little more if they see each other a little less.

****

II. ELEMENTARY SCHOOL AGE

School and Learning

Son Does Fast, Careless Schoolwork

Dear Dr. Sylvia,

My son does fast, careless work at school, and both his teacher and I are disappointed at the quality of his papers. He's a bright child and I know he's capable of better work. I don't understand why he seems to be so anxious to finish quickly. What's his hurry?

Dad of Hurrier

Dear Dad of Hurrier,

When I ask elementary school-age children who the smartest students in the class are, they usually give me specific names. Then I ask them why they think those children are smartest. Almost every child says, "Because they're the first ones done."

There appears to be unanimous agreement among kids that "fast means smart." That explains why your son races through his work.

Perhaps you could share this column with your child's teacher. Although teachers are usually aware of the speed problem, both your son's teacher and you and his mother will want to specifically emphasize to him that speed is *not* the same as intelligence. Sometimes the best

creative thinking is actually done slowly, and children do process information at different rates.

Teaching children to take pride in the quality of their work, rather than the speed of completion, is an adult team effort. Parents and teachers will want to *say* it and *model* it, because otherwise it seems very intuitive to children to believe that they will appear smartest if they are the first ones done.

****

Role of Letter Grades
for Poor Reader

Dear Dr. Sylvia,

What role should letter grading play for children such as my son? He is a poor reader and has a difficult time writing. He is only in third grade and I'm afraid he will become discouraged by bad grades.

Caring Mom

Dear Caring Mom,

It is reasonable for teachers to grade children's achievement even as early as third grade. However, I think it would be better for your son and for all children if teachers also used *A* through *F* grades for children's efforts in each subject. Thus, your son might get a *C* for reading achievement and an *A* or *B* for reading effort.

He could feel encouraged by his effort grades until his achievement catches up. Of course, as he continues with good effort, achievement will automatically improve.

Any rewards that you or the school would choose to give can be attached to his effort grades. A student with average ability could thus attain honor roll awards by getting mainly *A* effort grades. Rewards for hard work won't cause children pressure and puts the emphasis where it should be placed. Adults don't walk around with IQ test scores on their foreheads, but people who do a little more, who take initiative, and who have positive attitudes toward work are promoted and rewarded because they accomplish.

You may also want to explain to your son that not all children learn to read or write at the same time, but almost all children who continue to work hard do learn to read and write.

You may want to tell your son the story about the race between the tortoise and the hare, where the slow and steady tortoise wins the race. You may also assure him that in the race of school, there are lots of winners, and all children who do their work regularly and conscientiously become winners in life.

If your son works hard and continues to find reading and writing difficult, do ask your school to evaluate him for any possible learning disabilities.

****

Eight-Year-Old is Poor Reader

Dear Dr. Sylvia,

My eight-year-old daughter is a poor reader, and her teacher suggested that I listen to her read aloud each night. She hates to read to me and fusses and argues about it increasingly. I want her to be a good reader, but this approach is clearly not working. I love reading and can't understand why she doesn't.

Reading Mom of Nonreading Daughter

Dear Reading Mom,

Please read on. First of all, you may want to ask your school to evaluate your daughter to determine if she has a reading disability. If that yields no explanation, you may wish to have your daughter evaluated at Family Achievement Clinic for a specific reading disability called Scotopic Sensitivity. It is a biological disorder which is typically inherited. Thus one parent or an aunt or uncle is likely to have a history of an early reading problem. Scotopic Sensitivity is helped dramatically by colored lenses. Different colors seem to work for different people. If there is no actual problem, these tips for helping reduce reading anxiety will surely be effective. As a matter of fact, even if your daughter has a reading disability, these suggestions are likely to encourage her to enjoy reading more.

1. Children should not be required to read aloud to parents at home. Parents' anxieties convey themselves to children. Most parents feel tense when poor readers read aloud to them. Children should read aloud only if they choose to do so. As adult readers, they will rarely find oral reading important.

2. Parents should read aloud to their children as long as their children enjoy it (eighth grade is not too old). This should not be seen as dependence but only as a form of real family enjoyment.

3. Permit children to stay up half an hour later at night if they're in their bed reading to themselves (children don't usually like to sleep; it's adults who do).

4. Encourage children to read whatever they like during that prebedtime. Don't insist they read grade-level material. Comics, cartoons, sports magazines, easy material, and books read multiple times are all good for building confidence. If they love reading they will expand their interests as their reading improves.

5. Encourage children to read stories while listening to tapes of the stories. Don't stand over them to be sure they're actually reading; eventually they will.

6. Model reading by keeping a book around which your children see you enjoying.

7. Encourage children to read to their younger siblings, provided those siblings aren't better readers than they are. They shouldn't do this in their parents' presence but alone with their sister or brother.

8. Ask your child's teacher to permit her to read aloud to a preschool or kindergarten group of children. The books are easy, and the simplicity of the reading and the receiving audience of small children will build your daughter's confidence and love of reading.

****

Defining Underachievement

Dear Dr. Sylvia,

I have heard that you talk about the Underachievement Syndrome. Could you explain what that is?

*Dad - I Wonder If I Have
An Underachiever*

Dear Dad—Perhaps You Do,

Unfinished work, disorganization, excuses about forgotten assignments and homework, a disinterest in most academic subjects, and the description of school as boring or useless are the initial indicators of Underachievement Syndrome. Other characteristics, such as poor study skills, uneven abilities, high creativity, lack of perseverance, perfectionism, and escapes to books, television, or video games may also be typical of underachieving children. Underachieving children may have average, above-average, and even gifted abilities but are not working to these abilities in school.

Underlying the surface characteristics which these children exhibit are two main characteristics. First, underachievers have not regularly experienced the relationship between their own personal efforts and educational outcomes. Second, they are so highly competitive that they don't dare take the risk of making effort for fear they will fail to meet their own high expectations.

Underachieving children often have expansive but unrealistic dreams but have not learned the discipline or goal setting required to arrive at those dreams. It is easier for them to make protective excuses than to risk carrying out the activities that would be necessary for fulfilling more realistic goals.

Children with Underachievement Syndrome have a great many bad habits which they have developed to protect their fragile self-concepts. They unconsciously manipulate the adults in their lives, both parents and teachers, in ways that keep them feeling safe in the short run but plunge them deeper and deeper into underachievement. During the time when they should be benefiting from the learning experiences of school, they direct their energies toward avoidance of learning. They manage to get parents and teachers to provide more help than they actually need (dependent underachievers), or they try to dominate adults by arguing, debating, and pushing limits (dominant underachievers). Adults who respond intuitively to underachievers will find that they only reinforce those harmful patterns. Counterintuitive responses are actually more helpful.

My book *Underachievement Syndrome: Causes and Cures* further explains how children fall into these underachievement traps and how parents and teachers can reverse the problems.

****

Son Who "Forgets"

Dear Dr. Sylvia,

My son has very good grades but constantly has late papers. He always states, "I forgot." How can I deal with this? Does he have some kind of learning disability?

Worried Mom

Dear Worried Mom,

Children who "forget" their homework rarely have memory problems. Ask your son if he can remember sports records or other areas which interest him. I feel very sure you will find that his forgetting his homework is unrelated to his actual lack of memory capability.

There are some organizational strategies which will assist him. First, he needs a strategy for remembering his assignments. Assignment notebooks may work well. Large spiral notebooks may be easier to keep track of than small notebooks. He may choose a different assignment memory plan of his own. Children who come to our Clinic often come up with their own creative ideas for remembering assignments. Since they've invented them, they are more anxious to defend their plan and tend to use it more effectively.

Second, he needs a regular study time and place, away from the traffic of the household, so that he may learn good study and work habits. Lying on his bed listening to music while studying or sitting with a parent

at the kitchen table are not good study habits. Once children have a regular study time and place, exceptions may be made for school or social activities.

After he has completed his schoolwork, you or his dad should look over his accomplishments so that you may examine the quality of his work. Encourage him briefly if he's done well, and ask him to redo or correct his work if it is poor. Parents shouldn't correct the work as a teacher would but should give it an overall look, at least until middle school. By then, most children should be able to manage on their own.

The next step after your parent review is to watch him put his homework papers into his backpack. If he puts his work away immediately after completion, it will be more likely to make it to school with him.

Your son may also want to invent his own strategy for storing his work for school. Some children prefer organizers or folders for each subject. Others use one folder for homework only.

If these strategies are not effective, ask his teacher to send a note home on days when all his work is in on time, so that you and your husband can let him know how pleased you are. I don't know how old your son is, but if he's a second or third grader, stars or stickers on a chart may help him to see how successful he's become. Baseball or football cards work well for third through sixth graders. First, try these approaches without stickers or cards, since it would be better if he could learn the responsibilities without rewards. My book *Underachievement Syndrome: Causes and Cures* has some other suggestions to use should you need a better understanding of your son's problem.

****

Motivating All-*A* Student

Dear Dr. Sylvia,

How can I motivate my daughter who receives good grades to work even harder, that is, not to be satisfied with minimal requirements even though these requirements give her As?

Parent of Gifted Girl

Dear Parent of Gifted Girl,

It is true that some children who get all-*A* grades should be challenging themselves even more and seem to arrive at those high grades with minimal efforts. If they are learning very little and are not exposed to a more difficult curriculum, they will probably have difficulty at a higher level of their education when the curriculum or competition becomes much greater than that to which they are accustomed.

First, you will want to share your observations with the teacher. Be prepared. That may not be easy. Some teachers may assume that parents of all-*A* students, who ask for more challenge for their children, are pressuring them. Here's a suggestion for what you might say to your daughter's teacher:

> *Mr. Edwards, my daughter really enjoys your class, but it seems to me that she does almost no studying or homework. In the future, could you consider some extra projects that would fit into your curriculum and would encourage some independent learning experiences? We'll be happy to encourage these projects at home if you could give us guidance as to how we can help.*

Please notice that in the sample conversation, the parent has pointed out the positive part of the child's experience and has suggested activities for the future, and not necessarily the present. That will give the teacher the opportunity to observe your daughter more closely and plan for the future without feeling as if you're blaming the teacher for the past.

Whether or not your initiative with the teacher is effective, also plan to have some home learning experiences with your daughter. You or her father can share in community learning or scientific experiments or nature opportunities which will encourage her learning and initiative. These opportunities also offer you the chance to model curiosity, perseverance, and task completion for her.

There are other community enrichment learning activities planned for children like your daughter who would benefit from further challenge. College For Kids, gifted learning centers, drama, music, art, gymnastics or dance instruction, religious instruction, and sports activities of all kinds provide a rich variety of learning activities for children. Don't let your daughter choose too many activities at once, or both you and she will feel overwhelmed.

Parents and teachers share the responsibility for encouraging children to accept challenges. You are correct that children should learn to explore and persevere even if their grades are not reflective of a problem. Do expect work and study from your daughter, but be sure to leave plenty of time for play and fun. Children learn a lot from play and should have time without specific chores to permit their imaginations and personal interests to expand.

****

Understanding Child's Boredom

Dear Dr. Sylvia,

Is being bored at home the same as being bored at school?

Mom Who's Bored With Hearing About Boredom

Dear Bored Mom,

Boredom may mean different things to different children, whether they use the term at home or school. When children say they are bored, they often do not even understand the reason for their uneasy feelings.

At home, children may say they're bored if there are no friends around to play with or if they are required to do a difficult chore. Boredom may be used to describe their feelings of wishing to play Nintendo® or watch television when you've limited those activities. It may represent their missing a parent or sibling who is away. Sometimes it may only mean that they expect to be entertained.

Descriptions of school boredom may mean that children are not sufficiently challenged or in some cases, too challenged. If small muscle coordination, as in writing, is a problem for a child, he/she may describe schoolwork as boring because writing is difficult. Sometimes children describe school as boring because they'd rather be playing baseball or watching television.

When children express boredom frequently, it should indicate to parents that there is a problem. However, interpreting the cause of the problem will take parent and teacher observation. In some cases, the problems could be solved by changing curriculum in school or activities at home. In others, parents and teachers simply need to teach children how to take the initiative to dissipate their boredom independently. There is no simple solution for curing boredom for children, but perhaps the worst solution is to too quickly believe that the blame should be placed on someone other than the child.

In some ways, the most important gift we can give to children is the capability of coping with boredom in imaginative and productive ways. When all is said and done, all persons invest some time in boring tasks and responsibilities. Learning to make the most of boring tasks takes the ultimate in creativity. You and your child's teacher will want to decide separately whether activities should be changed by the adults or whether you should simply expect your children to invent their own cure.

****

Teaching Children School Responsibility

Dear Dr. Sylvia,

At what age should we expect our children to take sole responsibility for their homework, time scheduling, looking ahead for tests, etc? I have a third-grade daughter.

We Want To Do It Right

Dear Mom and Dad,

Children vary in their ability to handle homework independently. Third graders are likely to continue to require some guidance but certainly do not need very much help. Start your daughter with good habits by suggesting an appropriate time and place for her work. The time may vary depending on your family schedule, but she should be doing her homework before she watches television or plays Nintendo.® She is likely to want a snack and some outdoor play after school. Right before or after supper are often good times. If homework time is just prior to bedtime, she may be too tired or may dawdle to avoid going to sleep (children rarely want to go to bed; it is only we adults who desperately wish for bedtime).

Please don't sit with your daughter while she is working. Although you may wish to look over her work, there's no reason to correct it as a teacher would. If it appears satisfactory, tell her she's done good work. If it's sloppy and careless, tell her that "people in our family take pride in their work," and have her redo the work. Try to stay positive and encouraging. For example, you might say:

> *I hope you can finish your homework and do*
> *a good job so we can have time to play checkers*
> *or Scrabble at 7:00. I'll be looking forward to it.*

That statement fosters your daughter's partnership in work and play. Saying it in a negative way, "If you don't get your homework done, you can't play Scrabble with us," provides the same information. However, the negative statement is more likely to make your daughter angry and oppositional. It may prevent her from wanting to finish her work. She'll feel as if she's losing an argument. Many, many parents emphasize the negative and threaten their children regularly. These continuous threats prevent children from feeling trusted and good about themselves.

However, don't be too hard on yourself if every once in awhile you find you're being negative or overreacting. The frustrations and pressures of parenting may cause all parents to occasionally find themselves acting more negatively than they'd like. Be positive as much as you can. Middle and high school students should be doing all their work independently unless they have had a history of underachievement problems. In that case, parents may have to check or supervise a bit more closely.

Parents of children of any age may still quiz children in spelling, math facts, foreign language, etc., or may look over their written work if their children ask for assistance. Feel free to give them some study tips or explain concepts they don't understand.

A most important caution is: Don't let your interest in your children's education lead you to doing too much for them. You should permit them the independence and the privilege of experiencing struggle. They'll require struggle to grow in self-confidence. If you do too much, you steal their struggle and their opportunity to earn their self-confidence. That may sound harsh, but consider the way you grew in your own self-confidence. Experiences that are easy can be fun, but they do little to make you feel good about yourself. You realize that anyone can accomplish easy tasks. It's when you take the risk of attempting a difficult task and find that you can ac- complish something you never believed you could that you grow in self-confidence. Permit your children the wonderful sense of accomplishment that comes with ear- nest effort and perseverance. Someday, they'll appreciate the struggles you allowed them to experience and will earn that well-deserved self-confidence.

****

Boy Uncommunicative, Mopey, and Unhappy in School

Dear Dr. Sylvia,

My son, age eight (Grade 2), comes home from school happy. Yet I get reports from his teacher and class mother that he seems "uncommunicative, mopey, and unhappy." Should I be concerned? He says he likes school a lot.

Confused Dad

Dear Confused Dad,

My response may temporarily increase your confusion since my answer is both yes and no. I'll answer the "no" first.

No, you shouldn't need to worry about school being a bad experience for your son since he seems enthusiastic and positive about his day. If he is learning well and enjoying school, he is undoubtedly happy.

The "yes" is not quite as simple; however, neither is it a major problem. Your son would probably benefit from learning some simple social skills which would communicate better to others that he's happy.

The first easy lesson is teaching him to smile more. Suggest that he look at himself in the mirror when he is smiling and when he is not smiling, and ask him which he likes better. Suggest also that he look around at other students in the class to notice that smiling kids seem friendlier and more pleasant to be around. An occasional compliment from you, his mom, or his teacher will

reinforce the smiling. You could say, "You look so happy when you smile." *Don't* notice or pay attention to his frowns.

Also, it would be good to teach him to communicate. Arrange for his teacher to give him a token for each time he contributes in class. She could tally these on her desk and give them to him at the end of the day. He may bring the tokens home, and you can praise him for his good participation or permit him to save his tokens toward some special weekend treat. This will become effective rather quickly, and once he begins speaking up, it will become a good habit. You'll then be able to discontinue the tokens. One caution: The teacher should arrange the token activity with your son privately so that other children are not aware of his reward system. It won't be as effective if other students know about the plan. Secret plans work better.

You and your wife may also want to notice your own facial expressions. Sometimes children mirror their parents' smiles or frowns; the more you smile, the more he will.

In summary, your son is probably quite happy, but it is an important social skill for him to reflect his good feelings in the classroom and for him to participate in classroom discussion. You may be surprised at the rapid change in his demeanor as you make these few changes for him.

****

Gifted Son is Bored,
Unorganized in School

Dear Dr. Sylvia,

The preschool teacher recommended our son be kept in preschool for another year. We ignored her recommendation and are pleased to see his progress. However, all other teachers from kindergarten to fourth grade have complained that he is not very organized and is not listening carefully. During his first and second grades, he was punished severely by his teachers and also by us. However, his third-grade teacher recognized his talent, and now he is in the gifted program. My question is whether his continued inability to organize his work and listen carefully would have any adverse effect on his academic learning. My son complains that he gets bored and that he never learns anything in class. Do you have any other suggestions to help our son?

Confused Dad

Dear Confused Dad,

It is difficult for me to know if your son is truly unchallenged although he describes school as boring. Boredom can mean different things for different children. It can mean that the curriculum is either insufficiently challenging, or it can mean that it is too challenging. It may only mean that your son would prefer playing baseball or watching television or being with his friends. I would suggest that you make a request to have the school psychologist or a private psychologist test your son to determine if the curriculum is appropriate for his abilities. The psychologist can then work with your son's school if any curriculum change is determined to be appropriate.

As to his lack of listening skill and his disorganization, punishment at home or school will do nothing to help these problems and may make him more determined to oppose his teachers and his parents. He may need some guidance, some practice, and even some small rewards for improvement. Here are some suggestions for improving listening skills in a television world:

1. Encourage your son to listen to sports events or other programs on the radio (instead of watching TV).

2. Buy him some cassette tapes with stories or books to which he can listen.

3. Ask the teacher to write homework instructions on the blackboard so that if your son misses some oral instructions, he has a visual reminder. This will help other students as well.

4. Make lists with your son of chores or home responsibilities so he may check them off as he completes them.

5. Write him personal notes asking him to accomplish special responsibilities; and when you're pleased with his accomplishments, write him notes of appreciation and pleasure.

6. Monitor your son's television time. Be sure he is selective and limited in the amount of time he can watch television or play Nintendo.®

Now here are a few tips for organization. You will find others in my book *How to Parent So Children Will Learn*:

1. Purchase two-sided folders for every subject. Your son may wish to draw, paint, or "fancy" letter his folders to help him identify each subject.

2. All homework papers that are unfinished should be put on one side of the folders. When papers are either completed to bring to school or graded to bring home, they should go on the other side of the folder.

3. Once a week, go through all folders with your son, tossing any unnecessary papers and keeping special ones for the refrigerator door or a storage drawer. That will give him a fresh start each week.

4. At night after homework time, all folders and equipment should be placed in his book bag ready for his next day in school.

Teaching your son some regular organizational habits will surely be helpful. If you and your wife can make your own organizational techniques obvious to your son, that too will help him learn. Sometimes, for disorganized children, one parent is also very disorganized, and power struggles about organization take place between parents. That can also cause your son problems.

Since he's only a fourth grader, if you help him learn listening and organizational skills now, in a very positive way, his future in school can be much more successful. If you discover that he could use a more challenging curriculum in some subjects, that may also help.

****

Son Bored in School and Wants Parents to Teach Him at Home

Dear Dr. Sylvia,

I have a seven-year-old who says he's quite often bored at school. In speaking with the teacher about this last year, she suggested that he at least should do the expected material first before she can offer any kind of enrichment material for him. He refused because he says

it's too boring and easy. In the meantime, at home he wants us to teach him more addition and subtraction and proceed. I'm worried that if we teach him things beyond what he's doing in school, we'll just increase the discrepancy between what's expected there and what he's trying to do. Do you have any suggestions?

Parents Who Are Worried
About Teaching

Dear Worried Parents Who Are Teachers Too,

You have a dilemma which is not as strange as it seems. Your son enjoys learning from you more than he enjoys learning in class. Children describe school as boring and easy for many reasons, so we can't necessarily assume he isn't being challenged in school. We really don't know if his refusal to do his regular schoolwork is related to an unchallenging curriculum or to his wish for more individual attention. Your son may be asking for the opportunity to learn more from you as a way to keep your attention. Nevertheless, learning is a positive attention-getter, and if your son truly wants to learn from his parents, it would be wrong to turn him away.

My plan is to help him to conform to teacher expectation and learn from you as well. If he accomplishes this, his teacher will also recognize his wish for enrichment in the future.

Set up some special study time for your son at a desk in his room. Explain that he must first accomplish his expected "easy" schoolwork for your inspection. After you've reviewed his assignment, agree to spend some time showing him how to do some more advanced work. Each time you teach him an advanced concept, give him a small assignment so that he can work on your assignment independently and can show it to you afterward.

If you use this approach, you'll give your son a clear message of respect for his teacher as well as an opportunity to work ahead with you. Furthermore, he'll practice doing independent work for both you and his teacher. If he is willing to participate in this kind of learning program, the teacher will soon value his accomplishments and his positive attitude about learning. She/he will undoubtedly wish to enrich his school curriculum as well. Most of all, we all want your son to love learning and to value independence and perseverance in the learning process.

****

IQ Tests for Children

Dear Dr. Sylvia,

At what age is an IQ test helpful? Are there better types of tests and some that are not as good?
Mom and Dad Who are Confused
About Testing

Dear Mom and Dad,

Many parents are confused about IQ testing. The initials IQ stand for Intelligence Quotient. The term came from tests that were initially created by Alfred Binet in France in 1905 for the purpose of predicting whether children were sufficiently intelligent to benefit from schooling. He included a series of tests for children at each year of development and, based on the successful completion of tests, calculated their mental age and compared it to their chronological age. He multiplied that number by 100 to arrive at the intelligence quotient. Thus, children with IQ scores of 100 were considered average, those whose scores were below 100 were below average, and those above 100, above average. He established categories of scores to which he gave names varying from Imbecile to Genius and used these scores for making predictions about children's learning abilities. IQ tests have been changed and revised many times since Binet's first tests, and educators have become much more sophisticated in their use. Although they are often still referred to as intelligence tests, we now know that they only measure some kinds of intelligence and that scores are affected by cultural environments and learning.

Despite the many problems of IQ tests, we can still use them cautiously to predict how well children will do in various educational environments. They also permit us to identify strengths and weaknesses in children's learning styles. Individual IQ tests administered by a psychologist are much more effective than group tests, but even the latter can provide helpful information.

IQ tests can be helpful from about age four, but scores are less reliable for preschool children than for school-age children. The only reason to have a child tested as early as age four is if parents believe that the child is unusual. If your child is spontaneously reading or has mastered math concepts very early, an IQ test can be used to help you consider early entrance to school. If your child seems to be struggling with early home learning, the IQ test can help you decide whether he or she needs a special preschool program.

Group IQ tests are typically administered by schools in second or third grade, and teachers usually explain these scores to parents. The main purpose of IQ tests is to determine if children need either further intellectual challenge or special remediation. Despite their real limitations, IQ tests can be very helpful in making education decisions for children.

So to answer your question, if you are feeling uneasy about the appropriateness of your children's school achievement, ask your school or a private psychologist to evaluate their IQ to help you determine what is educationally best. However, if your children seem reasonably challenged and happy in school and their teachers agree with your perceptions, there probably is no need for any special IQ testing.

****

Attention Deficit-Hyperactivity Disorder (ADHD)

Dear Dr. Sylvia,

Do you find a correlation between underachievers and children with Attention Deficit-Hyperactivity Disorder (ADHD)? I seem to work with a group of underachievers who test high for ADHD.

Frustrated Teacher

Dear Frustrated Teacher,

ADHD children are difficult to teach and difficult to parent, and most of them also underachieve in school. However, not all underachievers have ADHD.

ADHD is characterized by high energy, difficulty with concentration, distractibility, impulsivity, disorganization, and a large number of the characteristics which are typical of many children with Underachievement Syndrome. However, all tests for ADHD are observational and behavioral. There are no biological tests for ADHD, although many persons conclude that a score based only on parent or teacher observations is like the result of a blood test for diagnosing ADHD.

The symptoms of ADHD can be caused biologically or they can be caused environmentally. I don't consider it appropriate to treat these symptoms with medication unless parents and teachers have worked with these

children behaviorally. High-energy children have always been harder to parent and teach, but high energy is also (although not always) a characteristic of intellectual giftedness.

Ritalin is the medication most frequently used for ADHD children. I believe that it is often overused and misused. One teacher of gifted children in Florida reported to me that half her students were being medicated for ADHD. Although Ritalin may calm and benefit a great many children, it would seem better to me if these children could learn to focus attention and discipline themselves toward motivation. Ritalin does have side effects for some children including loss of appetite, insomnia, stomachaches, headaches, and tics.

When we work with ADHD children in our Clinic, we find great success if parents and teachers are guided in setting clear limits for children. Teaching adults to take charge and to not overreact is helpful. Consistency between parents is extremely important. There are also techniques for teaching children to help themselves to concentrate and avoid impulsiveness and behavior problems. Many of the symptoms of ADHD can be controlled behaviorally. Thus, medication can be avoided for most of these children. A few of them will need both medication and behavioral help to work to their abilities in school. Teaching these children to achieve in school is certainly part of the cure.

In the past few years there has been a growing interest in Attention Deficit-Hyperactivity Disorder. Unfortunately, one sad result is an overdiagnosing of the disorder by parents, teachers, and professionals. It is almost as if Ritalin has been hailed as a magical cure. I have never found Ritalin to be a magical cure for Underachievement Syndrome. Underachievement is too complex a problem to be cured by a "wonder drug," and can be reversed when parents and teachers work together. While reversing underachievement takes time and perseverance, the side effects are positive for the child and the family, and the children do not become dependent on medication.

****

Boy With High IQ
Doesn't Like School

Dear Dr. Sylvia,

What can I do for my son's education? He is seven years old and in second grade. His IQ is 155+ (off charts). He was at sixth-grade reading level and did simple algebra in kindergarten. He has never liked school. He says he doesn't learn anything. His teachers have to push him to complete his assignments. We can't afford private schooling. He often has unexplained

sadness. He reads novels at home, 200 pages a night. He feels he's learned nothing in school in three years. I am a teacher and I try to encourage him, but I feel he's very sad about school.

Sad Dad of Sad Son

Dear Sad Dad,

There is good reason for you and your son to feel sad. Since school has never challenged him academically, he probably feels completely isolated socially as well. He may need some radical acceleration in basic subjects and may even require grade skipping.

Start by asking the school to provide a full evaluation of his ability and achievement. Hopefully, they will be pleased to help you since the problem is undoubtedly obvious to them. If the school psychologist doesn't have the time, go to a private psychologist who specializes in working with gifted children.

In your son's case, the next step could be total grade skipping or skipping a grade in only one or two subjects. I usually recommend no more than one grade at a time to permit adjustment. The sense of moving forward to more stimulating work is likely to serve as a motivator. It may actually be necessary to individualize mathematics if that is one of his strengths. On the other hand, individualizing reading could destroy his opportunities for discussion with other children, so it would be better to find an appropriate reading group for him, even if it is with slightly older children.

Despite his very high IQ, there is much for your child to learn. Acceleration research indicates that very gifted children may be happier academically and socially if they skip some grades. *Education of the Gifted and Talented* (Davis & Rimm, 1989) includes a chapter on acceleration strategies. Reprints of my articles on acceleration are also available upon request. Although it is impossible to make specific recommendations for your son based only on your question, changes should surely be made soon before he "turns off" to school learning in a more permanent way.

****

Family Relationships and Discipline

Daughter's Room is a Mess

Dear Dr. Sylvia,

What is the importance of children keeping their rooms clean? What is the best way to get my daughter to keep her room clean (or at least halfway)? I can't seem to convince her. Her room is a mess!

Mom Who's Not Sure It's Worth It

Dear Mom,

There are times when no mom is sure it is worth her effort, and you will personally need to decide how important it is to you. It is good for children to learn to take on responsibilities around the house that match their developmental level. They can learn to pick up their toys and even their clothes before they are two and can expand those good habits each year. Of course, they need to be patiently and consistently taught, and that can be so frustrating to parents that they find it more efficient to take the responsibilities on themselves. Unfortunately, children also learn that if they frustrate their parents sufficiently, the tasks will get done for them. Thus some bad habits begin.

The cleanliness standard for children's rooms doesn't have to match the standard for the rest of your home, but

it should meet some reasonable threshhold level so that 1) you're not embarrassed to bring a friend past the children's rooms, and 2) your children will become accustomed to a reasonably organized and clean environment.

Sit with each child and make a list of chores for which he or she should be responsible. Most families want beds made, clothes put in the laundry, and toys picked up. Some families include vacuuming and dusting, bathroom cleaning, or other household tasks on their list. Be sure your children have received your "how to" instructions for each task on the list. Explain to your children that you will not nag or remind but will inspect each Friday at five (or a time that would be convenient for you). You will expect all listed activities completed before weekend activities begin. That means no television, Nintendo,® inviting friends over, or visiting friends until their work is finished. Stay calm, firm, and consistent until they have developed good habits.

Some parents may choose a daily inspection before evening television. Some parents give their children an allowance only after inspection. An effective plan includes a specific list of activities, an exact time for accountability, and consistent follow-through by parents until the good habits are formed.

Room-cleaning problems stem from inconsistency and nagging without follow-through (a problem to which all of us are vulnerable). If you've been remiss, you're not alone, but don't be surprised to hear your children debate with you about their rights to live in their rooms the way they want them. Since children don't pay rent and parents do (or a mortgage payment), it does establish that parents may still have reasonable control within their own home. However, do be reasonable in setting children-comfortable expectations. If you set your cleanliness standards too high, your children will fight you, and you will find yourself wondering if it's worth the struggle.

Here's another tip to help your daughter. If her room is really out of hand, work side-by-side with her to organize it and clean it up thoroughly. That will make her feel like she has "a fresh start" and will encourage her to maintain the cleanliness. The side-by-side work can be fun and will give her a sense of your partnership instead of her feeling embattled with you.

As an adolescent I remember wondering why it was so important to my mother that I hang up my coat instead of leaving it on the nearest chair. Hanging coats was just not on my agenda, and I truly did not understand her point at the time. She persevered and I finally learned; then I persevered and our children learned. The real agenda is responsibility and reasonable organization—the requirements for effective accomplishment at home, at school, and in the workplace. Your daughter's room is a good place for her to start.

****

Daughter is Slow Moving
in the Morning

Dear Dr. Sylvia,

How can I get my daughter to get up and dressed in the morning without yelling or being late? We've tried getting up earlier and giving stars for being up and dressing on time. Sometimes that works and sometimes it doesn't.

Morning-Exhausted Dad

Dear Dad,

This is a question parents ask me frequently, so I can share my morning routine from my book *How To Parent So Children Will Learn* with much confidence. If you adhere to it regularly, school mornings will become a pleasant habit for your daughter, and you'll be able to send her off to school smiling.

"HOW TO" - FRESH MORNING START!

1. Announce to your children the guidelines for the new beginning. From this day forth, they will be responsible for getting themselves ready for school. Your job will be to await them at the breakfast table for a pleasant morning chat. The purchase of a new alarm clock may usher in the new routine. Children as young as four may use their own alarm clock.

2. Night before preparations include laying out their clothes, getting their books ready in the book bag, and setting the alarm early enough to allow plenty of morning time. They will feel just as tired at 7 a.m. as they will at 6:30, but the earlier start will prevent their usual rush.

3. They wake themselves up (absolutely no calls from others), wash, dress, and pick up their rooms (as itemized in checklist). Breakfast comes only when they are ready for school. Absolutely no nagging!

4. A pleasant family breakfast and conversation about the day ahead! Parent waits at the breakfast table and is not anywhere around them prior to their meal together.

Question: What happens if they don't dress in time for breakfast?

Answer: No breakfast. (That will only happen once or twice for children who like to eat).

Question: What happens if my children don't like to eat breakfast?

Answer: Fifteen minutes of television after breakfast, when they're ready for school, will probably be effective.

Question: What happens if they don't get up?

Answer: They miss school and stay in their room all day. That will happen no more than once.

Question: What happens if they don't have enough time in the morning?

Answer: They go to bed 30 minutes earlier and set the alarm 30 minutes earlier until they find the right amount of time necessary for independent mornings.

Question: What happens if I have to drive them to school or day care on the way to work?

Answer: Insist that they are in your car on time, in whatever state they are. They may finish dressing in the car or on the bus. Stay calm. They'll get the idea.

Question: Does this routine work?

Answer: *Always* with elementary-aged children. *Sometimes* with high school students. *Never* with high school students who like to skip school.

Dad, just in case you're feeling lonely with your problem, I do want you to know that this morning dilemma is one of my most frequently asked questions. You may feel lonely, but you are definitely not alone. Please repair the problem before high school. It can be a life-long, difficult habit thereafter.

One more small but important tip. Are you or her mother modeling "I'd rather stay in bed" behavior daily? If so, you or she may want to change that example. If you can show your daughter how to be a morning person, the entire process will change more quickly.

****

Children Act Up When
Mom is On Phone

Dear Dr. Sylvia,

Why do my children act up and become noisy as soon as I get on the telephone? What can be done?

Frustrated on Telephone

Dear Frustrated on Telephone,

So many parents have asked me that question that it almost seems as if the children in our world have a conspiracy against their parents' telephone use. Your children probably resent your giving someone else your total attention. Actually, a parent's right to communicate with other adults, either for business or pleasure, needs to be preserved within reason. Here are some rules you may wish to share with your school-age children:

1. Mom and/or Dad have the right to talk on the telephone without being interrupted by any children unless there is an emergency.

2. If there is an emergency, apologize first, then explain to us the emergency message.

3. If you want to communicate a nonemergency message, you may write it down on a pad so you don't forget to share it with us later.

4. You may continue to play while we're talking provided you are not arguing or shouting.

5. If arguing, shouting, or interrupting occurs, I'll ask my caller to wait for a moment and remind you to go to separate rooms quietly.

6. If you don't do that immediately, you'll owe me free time at bedtime. That is, you'll go to bed 15 minutes earlier for each time you interrupt our telephone conversations. (At least that will give parents more free time at night.)

Other Suggestions and Cautions:

1. If you are fortunate enough to have a portable telephone or a telephone extension in your bedroom, tell the children where you'll be talking, go to your room, and close the door. You may even want to design a sign to hang on the door to remind children not to interrupt.

2. Save most of your social telephone talk for when your children are at school or lessons. After all, time with your children is both limited and valuable. They and you need time to enjoy each other's attention.

3. For very young children, you may have to put them in their crib or playpen long enough to finish your phone call.

4. Don't interrupt your own phone conversation to answer your children's questions (unless they are of an emergency nature). Your permitting them to interrupt you is what continues the problem. The more you become involved with them while you're talking, the more they believe they have the right to interrupt. Be firm!

****

Son Won't Leave Play to Come to Dinner

Dear Dr. Sylvia,

How can I get my 11-year-old son to leave his play to come to dinner? He seems to need many reminders and comes only when I lose my temper.

Nagging Mom

Dear Mom,

Kids often have their own agendas and don't tune in to parents' calls. Some techniques you may try to avoid constant nagging follow:

1. Give your son a 15-minute warning that playtime will be over and dinner will start soon.

2. Call him only *once* at dinnertime. Then begin your family meal without him. When he arrives at dinner late, go on eating as if he has always been there. Don't make any special effort on his behalf, and don't talk about his lateness.

3. Does your spouse respond when you call him to dinner? If not, your son may be copying a family routine. Give your spouse a 15-minute warning, and then, confidentially, ask that he be "enthusiastically" on time. Number three may be even more important than numbers one and two.

****

Motivating Child to Stay on Task

Dear Dr. Sylvia,

What can I do to positively, gently motivate our eight-year-old to keep him on task? He does get distracted.

We Don't Want To Be
Nagging Parents

Dear Nagging Parents (but don't want to be),

It would certainly be important to teach your eight-year-old to take responsibility for task completion and to avoid having him get into the habit of becoming dependent on your nagging. While some distractibility is quite normal for any eight-year-old, it sounds as if his distractibility is attracting more of your attention than his task completion.

Parent paces have become quite hectic in households where both parents work. When there is not enough time, the slow pace of an eight-year-old may be quite frustrating. Planning enough time for your son to finish his responsibilities may be part of the problem. Waking him a little earlier, starting his bedtime "ceremonies" sooner, and allowing more time for his chores may help.

Teach him how to organize tasks by making lists of steps toward completion and charts to check off his progress. Checklists for morning routines, chores, or bedtime routines (see my book *How To Parent So Children Will Learn*) should be arranged with the more

boring steps first and the best steps last. Thus breakfast, storytime, or games should follow dressing, washing, etc. These routines become self-motivating because they provide your son with an actual goal to encourage him through tasks, and he won't require your regular reminders.

If he tends to move too slowly, he's old enough to learn to use a stopwatch to time himself. He can write his time down on his daily chart to see if he can beat his own record. The timing makes a fun game of his daily activities, and you will soon find you can praise his improved speed.

When you talk to his grandparents or each other about him (referentially), and he is within hearing, be sure not to use terms like "pokey" or "lazy" or "slow." He will assume he can't do anything about his problem. Instead, describe to other family members how much more organized, persistent, and responsible he has become. He'll soon live up to these new expectations, and charts will become unnecessary.

****

Angry, Frustrated Son

Dear Dr. Sylvia,

My nine-year-old son gets frustrated, angry, and quits when he can't "get it right the first time." How do I help him understand that mistakes are a part of the process?

Puzzled Mom

Dear Puzzled Mom,

It sounds as if your son's frustration and anger may be attracting a fair amount of your attention, and while his efforts and perseverance may not be rewarding to him, his lack thereof has effectively engaged you.

If you have explained to him over and over again about "learning from his mistakes," it probably won't help to repeat the lecture. He's heard you. Instead, when he loses his temper next, stay away from him and don't engage in any conversation. He may feel even angrier when you ignore his fuss, so if he follows you in storming protest, be prepared to quietly escort him to his room for some rest and recuperation.

At a different time which is unrelated to his tantrum, together compose a list of alternative techniques for handling his frustration. Let him know that he may choose from this list only. The list may include:

1. Temporarily discontinue the activity and return to it later.

2. Permanently discontinue the activity because it may be too difficult.

3. Relax on his bed for a few minutes with eyes closed until he feels in better control of himself.

4. Punch his pillow.

5. Take a walk or run, and return to work afterwards.

Let him know that if his tantrum becomes uncomfortable to anyone else at home, and he doesn't choose a technique which you've listed together, you'll quietly escort him to his room where he may stay until he is relaxed, after which he may come out.

Also change the praise words you use for your son's accomplishments. Choose words like deep thinking, persevering, patient, and creative when you describe his efforts. Avoid overpraising with words such as brilliant, extraordinary, perfect, amazing, and speedy. He may be internalizing overpraise as pressure and may feel frustrated because he can't measure up to expected accomplishment.

Also, when you talk to other adults, e.g., spouse, grandparents, and friends, within his hearing (referential speaking), don't refer to his tantrums or impatience. Instead, look for ways to comment on his increased persistence and problem solving. Your referential speaking to other adults sets expectations for your son, and it is better to set those expectations positively and realistically.

Lastly, monitor your own impatience. How do you handle your frustrations? If you're finding yourself losing your temper frequently, you may want to construct your own list of alternative techniques. Your son will be watching you and his father for hints on how to cope with the frustrations we all feel.

****

Mom Worried About Close Aunt-Daughter Relationship

Dear Dr. Sylvia,

My sister has a very close relationship with my youngest daughter. Although in some ways it seems very nice, I feel worried that she may at times side with my daughter against me when I try to discipline her or when I expect her to help me clean up around the house. I'm not sure how to handle this tricky situation.

Caught-in-the-Middle

Dear Caught-in-the-Middle,

Some children are not only blessed with parents and grandparents who love them but also have a "favorite" aunt or uncle who adores them. Often that aunt or uncle doesn't have children of his/her own and has thus built an

especially close relationship with a niece or nephew. There are pleasures and pitfalls in your daughter's special relationship with her aunt.

For her aunt, it may permit her to experience a fulfillment in her own life which she might not otherwise experience. At holiday times, birthdays, and even special trips, she may enjoy the companionship of your daughter whom she loves and who loves her.

For some aunts and uncles, however, the joys are mixed blessings since they are also reminders that they will not or cannot ever have children of their own. For others, those blessings are only mixed with the relief that they chose not to have the responsibility or burden of actually parenting children of their own. The fun of being with their nieces or nephews only confirms for them that they've made the correct decision.

But most important, you would like to know the pleasures and pitfalls for your own daughter. Sometimes aunts and uncles without children of their own can give your children learning experiences, fun excursions, and even gifts that you may not have enough time or money to afford. Since you know that your sister is enjoying your daughter and that your daughter is also benefitting from this special opportunity, you can be pleased for your daughter and for your sister. Some aunts and uncles are wonderful role models for their nieces and nephews and share special skills or interests with them.

What are the risks of your daughter's special aunt relationship? Suppose your sister leads a life-style to which you would not like your child to be exposed; or what might happen if your child complains to Auntie about how hard you are on her, and she agrees with your daughter, taking her side against you? These would cause major problems for you and your daughter since you would be likely to feel torn between wanting to be a good sister and a responsible parent. Of course, you want to be a good sister, but most important, you want to keep the power to guide your daughter's life. If your daughter really does get your sister to side with her against you, your daughter may actually become very rebellious against you.

Here's the hard part! If, and only if, Auntie is a bad role model for your daughter, or if she interferes with your discipline, you should be firm and assertive. Here are some recommendations:

1. Keep visits between your daughter and her aunt brief and impersonal.

2. Don't allow long trips or large gifts.

3. Communicate to your sister the changes you expect of her if she wants to stay close with your daughter.

4. Be firm. This is your own daughter. Don't let anyone make you feel guilty about these difficult decisions.

For the most part, aunt and uncle relationships are wonderful experiences for your children. If high risks aren't there, consider your daughter fortunate to have this special aunt.

****

Competition Between Twin Sons

Dear Dr. Sylvia,

How do I handle twins (age 8½) when one child succeeds at most anything he does or perseveres until he does succeed, and the other, who has a difficult time learning new concepts and gaining athletic prowess, would rather quit than compete with his brother?

Desperate Dad

Dear Desperate Dad,

It's difficult to see one child growing up in the shadow of his brother and feeling inadequate because of his brother's success. The pattern which is so common between close-age brothers is only heightened between twins. Parents often tend to either compare the less adequate brother or feel sorry for him. Even if you make no comparisons, your sons will make them anyway and

assume you are making them. If you deny the differences to protect your nonachieving son, it will seem to your sons that you are not being truthful. Furthermore, the nonachieving son may use your protection to avoid failure, and that will easily get him into habits of avoidance that you have already observed.

It is better to tell your boy that it is possible that he was born with less intelligence and poorer physical coordination than his brother, and while he may not like hearing that, most kids wish they were smarter and better coordinated anyway. Even if his brother is better at most things than he, there are plenty of kids out in the world that are better than both of them. There are also lots of kids who are not as able as he. It is best to accept the fact that we all have disappointing limitations, but that provides no excuses.

The game of life or school or sports is to do the best you can and to pursue your own interests and talents so that you can make the most of them. It's not how smart you are that counts as much as what you do with those "smarts."

In addition to the aforementioned minilecture on competition, you'll want to be sure to give each boy some separate time with each parent. Whether it's for sports, chores around the house, or cultural adventures, while total family activities can be the norm, the twin who lacks confidence should not always need to function in his brother's shadow. Father and son activities are particularly important for each son separately, although that will surely be difficult for you, Dad. You probably enjoy having the more positive son around you all the time. Nevertheless, if you hope to develop a positive attitude in both your sons, each needs to be with you some of the time without the other.

Mothers are often the protectors of their less confident sons, so you'll want to show your wife this column so that she doesn't make the all-too-common mistake of feeling too sorry for your less ambitious boy.

Mom and Dad, your twins are a difficult challenge. Sometimes, it may feel like you're balancing on a seesaw. As you help one boy build confidence, it may frighten the other into nonperformance, avoidance, and anxiety. Both boys will need to learn the important lessons about competition that all of us learn in life. No one succeeds all the time. No one fails all the time unless they give up. The rules of good sportsmanship apply well to life, but children require help in generalizing these rules beyond the baseball diamond or football field—and guess what!-adults often struggle with the very same competitive issues. Mom and Dad, you may even wish to observe your own styles of coping with competition. Perhaps a few small changes in how your twins see you in competition will help them cope more effectively.

****

Too Persistent Son

Dear Dr. Sylvia,

We have a seven-year-old son who is very persistent in repeating requests after having been given a clear answer; for example: "Can I go out and play with my friends?" "No, we're going to be eating in five minutes." "But, Mom..." Eventually, we end up really losing our tempers.

Frustrated Mom and Dad

Dear Frustrated Parents,

Your son, who has the persistent habit of persistence, is undoubtedly successful in convincing you to change your mind about half of the times he tries. He may even follow you around the room and argue with you. Because you want to be flexible and fair, sometimes he convinces you that his reasons are better than yours. Now he just won't quit. Unfortunately, if this continues, he will become even more persistent and annoying as he gets older. Furthermore, the more frequently you lose your temper, the more convinced he will become that you are unreasonable parents, that you don't understand him, and therefore, by adolescence, that he should do what he wants without even asking you. You can avoid all that with a wonderful anti-arguing routine (which can be found in my book *How To Parent So Children Will Learn*) that families tell me changes the home battleground to a much more positive atmosphere. I'll share it with you below:

ANTI-ARGUING INSTRUCTIONS

1. When arguers come at you (they always choose an inconvenient time because they instinctively know you're vulnerable), remind yourself not to say yes or no immediately. Instead, after they've made their request, ask them for their reasons. If you've asked for their reasons, they can never accuse you of not listening. Also, you'll feel better by not cutting off their expressions of feelings.

2. After you've heard their reasons, say, "Let me think about it. I'll get back to you in a few minutes (or after dinner for a small request; later for a larger one)." There are three marvelous benefits to the second step of this arguing process. First, it permits you to continue to be rational (that's what you wanted to be when you accidentally trained your arguers). Secondly, it teaches children to be patient. Third, since arguers are often manipulative children, they know that since you haven't yet responded with either a yes or no, their good behavior increases the

likelihood of your saying yes. Therefore, while you're taking time to be rational and while they're learning patience, these lovely dominant children will be at their best behavior. How nice!

3. Then think about their request and their reasons. Don't be negatively biased by their pushiness. If your answer is yes, smile and be positive and enthusiasic. Arguers rarely see adults smile.

4. If your answer is no, and you do have the right and obligation to say no sometimes, then say no firmly. Include your reason as part of your refusal. Don't change your decision (for at least 90% of the times), and don't engage in further discussion. Don't let them make you feel guilty. It is healthy for children to learn to accept noes.

5. Remind them calmly that you've heard their request, you've listened to their reasons, you've taken time to think about them, you've given them your answer and your reason, and that the discussion is now over.

6. If they continue arguing, and they're below age ten and not too big, time them out in their rooms. If they're too big for you to time them out, you go calmly and assertively to your room and lock your door. If they beat on your door, ignore them. Relax with a good book. Finally, they'll learn that parents have earned the privilege of saying no. They'll also have learned that they may continue to have the opportunity to remain children. They may not appreciate the latter at the time. However, your home will become a more pleasant and positive place in which to live, and your children will find that you are positive, fair, rational, and not a wimpy parent.

Your son will quickly change his approach after you've consistently used this routine a few times. His "But, Mom..." or "But, Dad..." may return occasionally as a reminder of the battling days, but truly the home atmosphere will improve dramatically.

****

Being Firm; Discipline

Dear Dr. Sylvia,

By being firm, can you damage a child's spirit? What type of discipline do you recommend?

Sensitive Mom

Dear Sensitive Mom,

Firmness does not damage children's spirits. It provides them with the safety and security they require in order to take risks. They know that they can take chances on new ideas or activities because they have confidence that their parents will let them know if they've gone too far.

Rigidity and cruelty, however, can be damaging. Kids who live in fear of punishment have little energy for adventure or curiosity. Often when their authoritarian caretaker is not patrolling they do sneaky and naughty things.

Research suggests that authoritative (neither too authoritarian nor too permissive) parenting is best for children's growth and development. A positive but firm parenting style sets clear limits and gives good direction but doesn't dampen spirits. Parents shouldn't hesitate to take charge. You may appreciate this quotation from an article on gifted children which I wrote:

If God had meant gifted children to run our homes, She would have created them bigger.
(Rimm, 1984)

Perhaps you could view firmness as the important V of LoVe: Visualize the letter "V" as a model for guiding your children's power. When they're very young they begin at the bottom of the "V" with limited freedom and power. As they mature and are able to handle more responsibility, the limiting walls of the "V" spread out, continually giving them more freedom while still providing definite limits. During adolescence, as they move to the top of the "V," they become capable of considerable independent decision making and judgment but should continue to recognize that there remain adult prerogatives in guiding them. They are thus readied for moving out of the "V" into adult independence and personal decision making.

Now reverse that "V" so that it looks like this: "Λ." Children brought up at the base of this figure are given too much freedom and wide limits. They become accustomed to independent decision making before they're able to handle their freedom responsibly. As they move toward adolescence, parents become concerned that their children may misuse their freedom. They worry about the dangers that arise in school and community. Cigarettes, alcohol, drugs, and promiscuous sex are perceived as threats from which their children must be protected; so they begin to set limits. They take freedoms away. Adolescents who had too much control as children now feel overcontrolled by parents. Their statements echo their feelings of restriction. They complain, "My parents are controlling me. They used to treat me like an adult and now they treat me like a child!" They push all limits and oppose and rebel. They feel angry and depressed. They lie and cheat. Worried parents overpunish and narrow the limits further, resulting in even more rebellion. Ugly adolescence turns the formerly happy home into an armed camp. Once freedom is given, it isn't easily taken away. The "V"-shaped guidance is much smoother and more comfortable for children and parents alike.

Empowering children with adult decision making provides power without wisdom. It leads to formidable and continuing conflicts between children and their parents as they compete for the power that parents give too early and try to recover too late. The resulting adversary mode may force adolescents to rebel too stubbornly, parents to respond too negatively, and both to lose the positive home atmosphere that can be so valuable in educating children.

****

Daughter Competing With Gifted Older Sister

Dear Dr. Sylvia,

We have two girls, ages ten and eight, who are very competitive. The ten-year-old is gifted and tends toward perfectionism. Her eight-year-old sister is very bright, but just misses the gifted program cut-off. How do we deal with this area without making one feel superior and the other like she doesn't measure up? She (the eight-year-old) is very gifted athletically and excels in gymnastics while the ten-year-old doesn't. This doesn't compensate, in her opinion, for her sister being "smarter."

Frustrated Mother

Dear Frustrated Mother,

It is hard not to be sympathetic to your child who may not measure quite as high on an intelligence test as her older sister, but being too sympathetic will only make the problem worse. It is important for children to come to terms with the fact that there will always be others who are "smarter" than they are. They may also want to realize that no matter how "smart" one is, they are likely to wish they were smarter. If your younger daughter can accept herself within her limitations (which don't really sound very limiting), she will actually

discover that ability is not as critical in the world as what you do with that ability. There are all kinds of opportunities in our society for children who have a positive attitude, take initiative, are willing to work hard, and have developed many genuine interests. Adults don't walk around with a big "G" on their forehead for "gifted" nor do persons earn success by an IQ score. Suggest that your younger daughter stop feeling sorry for herself and instead get the most out of her school and home learning opportunities. As she works hard and gets involved, she will gain satisfaction from her accomplishments, earn good grades, and learn to love learning too. Her bright future does not depend on her doing better than her sister in school. She will accept herself better if you don't attempt to sugarcoat the truth.

As to your perfectionistic older daughter, you may as well warn her about the future. She may feel "smartest" in her family or her class, but "smartest" is only a temporary place. She too will need to know that in the world there are no "first" places but many opportunities to contribute if you are willing to risk not being perfect. Your chances for success narrow considerably if you are not willing to make mistakes and learn from them.

Mom, as to your younger daughter's gymnastic ability, she is absolutely correct that her talent in gymnastics is not likely to compensate for her intelligence, and it would help her if you level with her about that as well. Unless she is extraordinarily talented, she is unlikely to become a professional athlete or an Olympic gymnast. Encourage her to enjoy gymnastics for the fun of the activity and for the self-discipline and social opportunities it provides. Remind her that she doesn't need to be best in the family at anything to receive your love and neither does her sister, but you do want her to be the best she can be because, indeed, that will help her to feel good about herself.

****

Social and Emotional

Mom Concerned About
Ownership of Friends

Dr. Sylvia,

How can I convince my ten-year-old daughter that "ownership" of friends is not good when her present friends "assume" ownership of her.

Owned Parent

Dear Owned Parent,

You may first want to observe your daughter's friendships more closely. Are the tight relationships you're noticing truly "ownership" by one child, or are they only the normal close friendships which emerge temporarily at your daughter's age? Is your daughter initiating ideas and activities or only participating in her friends' suggested activities?

If you continue to believe your daughter's friends own her, your daughter may be too socially dependent. She may be willing to do what her friends want her to do despite the appropriateness of those activities. However, if you've already tried to convince her that ownership is too controlling and that hasn't worked, you probably will only make her angry by forbidding such a tight friendship.

Instead, suggest she invite other friends to your home occasionally without her "ownership" friend. Also set aside one weekend day as family day with no outside friends visiting. Plan with your daughter some summer camp experiences where she may meet all new friends and where none of her present friends are in attendance. Also, search out occasional weekend enrichment activities which involve other groups of similar-age children.

Ten-year-old girls tend to baffle their parents with their special friendship groups. They often have secret clubs with secret activities, secret letters, and sometimes even secret boyfriends. They may group together and isolate one girl and then join together with the isolated girl and isolate a different girl. They can be quite cruel to those they have isolated.

You can use this typical social style as a good tool for teaching your daughter to be sensitive and kind, to understand when she is hurting others, and to realize that her own hurt feelings may only be a temporary problem. The dual themes which will help to guide her are independence and kindness.

****

Socializing An "Only" Child

Dear Dr. Sylvia,

The idea of sibling rivalry doesn't really exist in our household because we only have one child, a ten-year-old daughter. The one thing that really bothers me most is that she really seems to have trouble with relationships with other kids. I guess because she's an "only" child, it makes it harder for her to socialize. What can we do to help her develop social skills?

Social Dad

Dear Social Dad,

"Only" children have some social disadvantages as well as almost as many advantages. They tend to be socially independent because they are accustomed to keeping themselves entertained. Be sure to recognize and value that quality in your daughter since it's often especially lacking in females. Social independence will be helpful to her in a career and in life.

However, "only" children are frequently unaccustomed to sharing both attention and power. You will want to observe your daughter when she has friends visiting to determine if her inability to share either of these cause some of her social problems.

Here are some suggestions to increase social sharing experiences. Invite a similar-age cousin (if there are any) to spend a week during the summer vacation with you, and hopefully, your daughter can exchange a similar cousin week at his or her home. Have her invite a friend to stay overnight occasionally on the weekend. Even numbers work out better and will avoid the problem of your daughter being the child left out.

Don't take your daughter with you to adult-only activities. Instead, leave her with a babysitter or, better yet, at a friend's house. She may be too accustomed to socializing with adults where she is easily included as one of the adults or just given too much attention.

Be sure that she joins some (not too many) social activities such as Girl Scouts, church or synagogue social groups, or school clubs. Definitely include a week or two of summer camp in your plans for her.

If your daughter participates in at least some of these activities, she will have ample opportunity to learn the comfortable social skills she may be missing at home. Single children have many advantages, so you don't need to feel guilty about depriving her of siblings. As she grows up, her social independence will become a greater advantage.

****

Is There Any Value of Nintendo®?

Dear Dr. Sylvia,

I have been working hard at decreasing the time my children spend in front of the "boob tube." For Christmas they received a Nintendo® from a relative. I realize that I have to strictly limit their time spent in front of it; but, tell me, is there any value to youngsters such as good eye coordination? I feel it's wasted time!

Persevering Mom

Dear Persevering Mom,

Please continue to persevere in monitoring your children's television watching, and please add to your thankless tasks the monitoring of Nintendo.® I'm sure your relative meant well, and I shall try, for your sake, to find some benefits of Nintendo.®

Like many other video games, Nintendo® may possibly improve your child's visual-motor integration. It may even serve to help them maintain some good concentration. If they play with others, it may serve to help them learn good sportsmanship. As your children improve in skill, it may increase some very specific confidence in Nintendo® playing. Furthermore, it serves as a reasonable form of punishment to be taken away for a day if their behavior has been inappropriate.

I hope, however, that I haven't been too convincing since a computer can provide all those advantages and many others and is definitely preferable to Nintendo.®

Unfortunately, there is a long list of disadvantages for Nintendo.® Some Nintendo® games are violent and seem to encourage aggressive behavior in children. Furthermore, children spend so much time playing these games, that it may seem difficult to lure them away for healthier outdoor play, their chores and responsibilities, reading and/or homework.

Since Nintendo® is here to stay for awhile, I suggest you reserve it for weekend play or until all chores and homework are completed. Even then, allowing only a reasonable amount of time for play (no more than 45 minutes to an hour) will minimize any damage and still permit your children to enjoy their relative's gift without major harm.

You're one of the few moms who cares so much that you're willing to set limits. Your children may not tell you that they appreciate that on a daily basis, but they will feel much more secure as a result. Keep up your good work.

****

Children's Summer Boredom

Dear Dr. Sylvia,

Now that summer's here, my children complain constantly of boredom.   There are no friends in the neighborhood, so they'd like me to taxi them to activities or friends' houses continuously.   I don't mind some of that, but shouldn't children be able to keep themselves busy **somtimes***?*

Tired Taxi Driver

Dear Taxi Driver,

Children should have some stimulation afforded by friends and activities during the summer, so you will undoubtedly want to invest some time behind the wheel to provide entertainment and fun.   However, it's also very healthy for children to learn to play alone for some part of each day.   Aloneness stimulates imagination, creativity, initiative, and independence.

You and your children may want to begin by brainstorming a whole list of activities they could do on their own.   Once the brainstorm list is completed, post it to inspire your children.   Insist they spend at least an hour a day without peers, siblings, or adults.   You may want to call that hour "independent time."   Don't allow television or computer games, but encourage them to choose any other activity, e.g., reading, writing, games, imaginative play, gardening, biking, arts or crafts, or just

daydreaming. Eventually children not only learn to enjoy their time alone but may even extend it beyond your suggested time. Some children will find the value of aloneness, but if you don't establish "time alone" as a routine, most will continue to believe they must have peer or adult entertainment. You will watch your children's confidence and interests increase when you put aside time for them to get to know themselves and explore their own interests.

****

Son Complains of Stomaches, Headaches Before School

Dear Dr. Sylvia,

We have a nine-year-old son in the fourth grade who is doing very well in school, has good rapport with his teacher, but practically every morning he has an upset stomach or a headache. We've taken him to our physician, and there's nothing wrong with him. We feel like we're punishing him by sending him off to school.

Mom and Dad Who Wonder
If He's Faking

Dear Mom and Dad Who Wonder,

Since you've already checked with a physician, you've taken the first and most important step. You've ruled out any problems that would actually require him to stay at home. However, he may truly be feeling the head or stomach pain, so please don't accuse him of faking.

Instead, explain to your son that when either of you have mild headaches or stomachaches, you still go to your job, and as you concentrate on your work, the pain often goes away. Explain that you expect him to go to school and concentrate on his work unless he has a fever. Suggest that if the pain gets too bad, and if he feels he'd rather rest for a short while, he could ask permission to go to the nurse's room to lie down for a few minutes until he feels better.

You shouldn't feel guilty about sending him off to school. On the contrary, you'd be doing him real harm if you permitted him to stay home on headache days.

Also, I would ask you to do some school research. Talk to his teacher about his complaint. Ask her to notice if he is being teased by any students. Peer harassment often causes tension which children may be afraid to tell their parents or teachers about. Cooperative learning groups sometimes cause stress for children who worry that the actions of other children in the group will lower their group grade. They often feel helpless about changing the situation or may feel intimidated by other more aggressive students in the group. Also check with your son's teacher about appropriateness of his curriculum. Is the work too hard, too easy, or too time-pressured? Ask the teacher if he/she thinks your son may need a few more positive strokes or some moderate praise to feel more encouraged or included. Finally, talk to your son's teachers about permission to go to the nurse's room for a brief rest should he have a headache or stomachache. However, be sure that the nurse in the room doesn't arrange to give him individual attention, or he may enjoy those visits too much.

If the problem continues, although that's unlikely, you may wish to arrange for group counseling in school or individual counseling by a private counselor. It is possible that there are more deep-seated issues, but minor anxieties usually disappear with the suggestions I've made.

****

Eight-Year-Old is a Worrier

Dear Dr. Sylvia,

What can I do to help my son balance the difference between his intellectual age and his emotional age? He's worried about death, religion, recycling, finances, and animal rights. He's only eight. He's worried and depressed. I beg him to let me to do the worrying, but it doesn't work. Help!

Worried Mom

Dear Worried Mom,

Your son certainly seems to show unusual concerns for an eight-year-old, and he is undoubtedly a bright and perceptive boy. I have three suggestions that will help him focus more of his thinking on more easily solvable, child-size problems.

As a kind, sensitive mother, you are probably directing your effort toward rationally discussing his worries with him in an attempt to ease his pain. However, since none of his worries are easily solvable, your discussions give him more facts and more sympathy than he is able to cope with. Certainly, we want you to be sensitive to his problems, but it would be better to answer him with a sentence or two, and redirect his conversation to more here-and-now activities which help him to understand how he can help others; for example, save money for a charity, collect cans for recycling, collect trash in parks, etc. By doing good things instead of only worrying, he can feel as if he's helping society.

A second suggestion is to monitor your discussions with other adults which are within his hearing (referential speaking). The more you talk about your worries about his worrying, the more he will worry. It is as if you have labeled him a "worrier," and he may believe that worrying is what he does best.

Third, and most important, his worries probably reflect your worries, and he probably hears you discussing problems with his dad or with friends and family members. Since he loves you, and his kindness and sensitivity are valued qualities, he may be taking on your problems in an effort to help. Try to discuss your problems more privately with as much optimism as you can muster. That will help him become more optimistic and positive about his world. Your offer to do his worrying for him will only exacerbate your son's oversensitivity problem.

Of course, we all want our children to be concerned about societal problems, but we adults and our children need to balance between protecting our families and our globe and the joy of living in our world.

****

Peer Pressure

Dear Dr. Sylvia,

My son's friends do poorly in school. He feels "out of it" if he does better than them; therefore, he does poorly in school. What should I do?

Dad Who Wants His Son
To Be Really Adjusted

Dear Dr. Sylvia,

What should I say to my child when he does something that is not acceptable and responds with, "All the kids do it?"

Mom Who Wonders Where
This Will Lead

Dear Dad and Mom,

Although your questions come from two separate families and are about two unrelated children, my response will help both of you. When children are in elementary school, parents and teachers alike worry a great deal (perhaps too much) about social adjustment and fitting in with the rest of the group. If children play alone or have only a few friends, both teachers and parents tend to encourage them to join others or invite friends to their homes almost as if they fear that children who are not popular will not be successful. If we continually redirect their independent activity to social activity, and we praise the more social children in the family or in the class, our children will receive a very strong message about social adjustment that leads directly to peer conformity.

By fourth or fifth grade, we find that children have learned our values well, and they repeat them back in a form which we prefer not to see. When the peer norm is "casual" and uncaring about schoolwork, our bright children who wish to "fit in" stop studying. Some children will copy, cheat, be disobedient, and even break the law to fit in with friends who are doing the same. When their dishonest activities are discovered, they ask their parents to excuse them based on fitting in with their friends.

Dad and Mom, you are asking about a very serious problem in our country. I know you don't want your children to be without friends, but these are crucial years for teaching your children your value system which I'm sure includes honesty and achievement. Don't "wimp" out because you or they are afraid of their losing friends. Let them know early and often that everyone has to go it alone at times in life. Tell them that it is more important to "stand tall" and know that they are living by a standard of excellence and honesty than to conform to a peer standard that in the long haul will cause them problems. Let your children know that it's all right to "walk alone" because it will equip them to be strong. Encourage them to be selective in their friends. A few good friends with similar values and interests are healthier than a crowd who may get them into trouble. Good academic habits and independence provide critical equipment for the rest of their lives. You may be interested in reading my article *Popularity Ends at Grade 12!*, which is available upon request.

****

Daughter Won't Take Risks

Dear Dr. Sylvia,

I have an eight-year-old daughter who is very reluctant to take any kind of risk in a public situation. She's actually very adventurous and creative and dynamic with the family or with close family friends. In taking classes, for instance, she will only take private rather than group lessons because she's afraid of failing in public. Even in school, in offering an answer in class or if she has a problem, she's very reluctant and hesitant to put herself forward to answer or ask for help. I'd like to promote more risk-taking. She's actually somewhat competitive too, but she's afraid of failing, so she doesn't want to join any kind of team or activity.

Mother Who Is Hesitant To Push

Dear Hesitant Mother,

While it is probably true that some children are inhibited from birth, all children can learn some increased risk-taking. Your first step is to remove the word "shy" from all conversation with or about your daughter. That often becomes a negative label for children, and whether you are addressing them directly or talking about them to other adults within their hearing (referential speaking), it feels like a limiting label.

Insist she participate in at least one group lesson or activity for health, safety, and physical fitness. Swim lessons, ballet, gymnastics, baseball, soccer, tennis, or basketball offer varying alternatives from which she may choose. Give her a time limit for making a choice and then sign her up. Drop her off at the activity and leave. Don't stay to witness her agony, and she will make less fuss. Ignore any tears; she'll recover. The activity will become a routine and will help her build confidence. Soon she'll be ready for another one.

Play competitive games at home, and be sure you don't always let your daughter win. If she withdraws and pouts, ignore the pouts, and go on having family fun. If she rejoins the game, count her in, but don't give any special notice to her joining you. If other family members tease her about being a poor sport, don't protect her. She'll soon learn to protect herself by overcoming her problem.

Take her aside at a different time and have a personal tête-a-tête with her. Tell her how pleased you are that she's overcoming her shyness and her fears. You may also want to mention to your husband and her grandparents her increased maturity, preferably within her hearing.

If she complains about problems in school, suggest she practice role playing a conversation for solving the problem. Together, brainstorm a few alternative solutions to the problem, and pretend you're the teacher. In the teacher's role, practice giving her possible positive and negative responses so she won't be too devastated if the teacher doesn't respond as she'd like. She needs to learn to risk accepting noes and realizing that she can't always please adults but, nevertheless, can continue to be assertive.

Finally, try to get her involved in some group competition. Some examples of group competition include Future Problem Solving, Odyssey of the Mind, music ensemble contests, and sports teams.

As she matures and progresses, she will develop the confidence to become involved in individual competition such as essay and art contests, individual music competitions, forensics, science fairs, and invention conventions.

Your daughter needs to take small steps forward, so please view these suggestions as a long-range plan with noncompetitive activity involvement first. As she progresses in confidence, introduce one new opportunity at a time. Most important, be positive. Focus your attention on her small steps forward, and try to ignore her regressions. Since her family involvement is so positive, you have good reasons to be optimistic.

****

Son Won't Give up "Buzz" Haircut

Dear Dr. Sylvia,

I have an eight-year-old in third grade who loves to have his hair "buzzed" (buzzed off with a clipper). He refuses anything else. He's had this hairstyle for a year. Is this all right?

Parents Who Disagree

Dear Disagreeing Parents,

Hairstyles are an age-old issue which varies only with the time and the length and style of the hair. The problem stems more from your parental disagreement than whether to buzz or not too buzz. At age eight, the haircut style can still be a parental decision, and you should be most concerned with the image the buzzed haircut style conveys about your son. If you see the image as negative, explain this to your son, and both of you should take a firm stand against it. If you view the image as positive, take a firm stand together for it (unlikely, I'm sure).

Most likely one of you sees the image as negative, and the other doesn't really like it but finds it mainly a harmless representation of your son's individuality. It sounds as if a compromise haircut is required—not a complete buzz but something both parents feel comfortable with and your son can accept.

If even one parent opposes the "buzz," under no circumstances should your son be allowed the haircut because the "buzz" then becomes a strong message of disrespect for the opposing parent with the support of the other parent. You are thus teaching your son rebellion against that parent and are being unfair to your spouse.

Expecting your son to conform to the strong wishes of both parents is not unreasonable; the parent united front will be helpful should he become angry with you about the issue. However, it is important that the easygoing parent does not sabotage the firm parent. Here's a conversational example of parent sabotage:

Son: I really must have a buzz haircut.

Mom: Well, I don't mind, but your dad objects, so I guess you can't do it.

That conversation makes Dad into an ogre, and even if the "buzz" doesn't happen, your son will resent his father. Respect each other, and either both agree to compromise or both deny or both permit the "buzz." United parents are much more important to your son than the haircut. If you want him to change the hairstyle, all you need to say to him is:

Mom: Neither Dad nor I like that "buzz," but we both sure like your hair when it's in a neat, short style.

Then follow through and the problem should disappear.

****

III. PRETEENS & TEENAGERS

School and Learning

Studying on Bed With Music

Dear Dr. Sylvia,

My daughter insists that she can only study on her bed with loud music on. She says she feels more relaxed that way and that her teacher told her class that kids should study in their favorite study style. My daughter's grades are poor. How can I convince her that studying in quiet is more effective?

Unconvinced Parent

Dear Unconvinced,

Your daughter may be more comfortable studying her favorite way, but comfort is not a measure of effectiveness; her grades are. You may want to point out that she will not be allowed to take her *SAT*s with music. Most schools don't permit students to work in class while playing music. She will need to learn to study in silence if she plans to be successful in school. Tell her that if she can improve her grades while studying quietly at a table or desk and has proven she can earn good grades, you can certainly permit her to experiment with introducing quiet music. If she can then maintain her good grades, she has proven she can study both ways.

****

Motivating Student to Get 'A's

Dear Dr. Sylvia,

*My ninth-grade son is doing reasonably well at school (As, Bs and an occasional C), but he's capable of better grades. How can I ask my child to perform **better** when he is already achieving **well**?*

Perplexed Dad

Dear Perplexed Dad,

It is difficult to tell from your question whether your son is underachieving by just a little or by a lot. Grades don't give me a total answer any more than they give you an answer. That's why you feel perplexed.

If your son is making a good effort by paying attention in class most of the time, handing in all his assignments, and studying reasonably for his tests, it is better to permit his maturity and personal motivation to guide him even if you wish he were studying a little harder. You may actually be pressuring him if you expect more. However, if there are some missing assignments, or if he does not study for tests, you should view him as an underachiever regardless of his grades, and you should not consider him to be achieving well even if he has *A*s and *B*s and an occasional *C*.

As a father, you are in a uniquely strong position to bring him in for a man-to-man talk. High school is very important. His grades will count toward college entrance and scholarships. The learning and study he will do in high school are extremely relevant to his preparation for college. Explain to him that capable high school students should be studying and doing homework for two to three hours a night. Help him plan a schedule to include at least that time frame. Put the plan in writing, and ask him to keep a daily record of his study time for each subject. Meet with him once a week to review and analyze his plan.

Ask yourself questions like these: 1) Are there changes in his study time or place that might work better? 2) Does he have the appropriate study techniques for each subject? 3) Is he going to the teacher for help when he requires it? 4) Does he need some organizational strategies for remembering assignments or for planning long-term assignments? You may be able to suggest some alternatives for his study program. Some helpful study suggestions are included in my book *How to Parent So Children Will Learn.*

Try to keep your communication to your son positive, and be genuinely interested in his progress. Be sure that his mother is backing you and being supportive of his schoolwork. On the other hand, it is better that you take the leading interest rather than she. As teenage boys approach manhood, it is very important that they receive messages from their father relative to schoolwork. Sometimes that is difficult for mothers to understand, and of course, if there is no father in the family, mother must be the son's guide. However, in your son's case, it appears that if he is underachieving, it is only to a slight degree. Your expressed concern and follow-up over a few months is probably all that will be necessary to let your son know that you take his schoolwork seriously, and, therefore, so should he.

****

Grandparents Concerned About Hyperactivity in Grandson

Dear Dr. Sylvia,

I read your article "Underachievers Hyper" in our newspaper and was extremely interested in it because our grandson, age 12, is having difficulties in school. The description of the ADHD fits him to a "T." He has been having problems for the past few years, but this last year was very bad and almost got him expelled. He has been punished, and detentions have been given, but nothing seems to work. Your article described the disorder but does not mention treatment. He needs help now before we lose him. Education is very important. We don't know what to do. His dad was told that since he attends a Catholic school, he is not qualified to get any help from

Social Services. No counseling is offered to him. They had talked about putting him in "special classes."

My question is: What help is available for children with Attention Deficit-Hyperactivity Disorder (ADHD)?
Concerned Grandparents

Dear Concerned Grandparents,

Your grandson does need help immediately. Children enrolled in private schools are entitled to evaluations by public schools, although they must go to the public school for the evaluation. Private psychologists will also be happy to help you.

Consistency and limit setting are two important skills which are helpful for parents to know for these children. The limit setting for a 12-year-old is best handled by the "Anti-Arguing Routine" and "How To Use Rewards and Punishments Appropriately" which I describe in my book *How to Parent So Children Will Learn*. Parents of ADHD children often find themselves overreacting and becoming very negative with their children. Then these same parents tend to feel guilty and contradict themselves and often give in to their children's wishes. Since parent limits are not clear, children seem to push constantly and don't learn positive self-control.

Another parenting problem which is very common for ADHD children is inconsistency between parents, with one parent being too strict and the other being protective. The same book I mentioned earlier explains how parents can compromise and form a united front and avoid what I call "Ogre and Dummy Games."

There are school changes that we make for ADHD children as well by explaining to teachers how to set limits. If ADHD children earn reputations for being "bad" kids, they often lose friends and feel picked on.

We have had much success with ADHD children, and I have included an excerpt from a letter from a mother whose son we helped recently. These children are somewhat harder to parent and teach, but they can almost always function in a regular classroom, and with appropriate help, they can be successful. The following letter was written by a parent of a boy who had been referred to my Clinic by a teacher because the teacher thought the child should be given Ritalin:

Dear Dr. Rimm:

*Just a quick note to share the excitement at our son's great progress after our visits with you. You gave us many tips such as Daddy being the primary one to "help with" homework, not to dwell on his inability to sit still in class but to tell him, simply, that it's what's expected of him, and the help we got with your **Learning Leads Q-cards**. Our son did want to try harder to be more attentive, and once he knew how important his being the best student he could be was, and that being a student is his most important job, we saw changes. His teacher has publicly said that he's most improved, and he's getting a* *"no uniform day" for good behavior for the first time in three years.*

Our parents' hearts told us that our very active boy was not a candidate for Ritalin despite the suggestion by the teacher. We understood her need for more cooperation and knew this route might be more work and effort for my husband and me, but the payoff of not having a child on continuous medication was uppermost in our intentions. And the results were that our parents' hearts were right! Dr. Rimm, your simple but most effective techniques prevented another needless case of a child on Ritalin when the alternative was and is so much better for the child. He has learned, we have learned. We're glad you were there for us and for our son. Thank you, thank you.

One more note. This is a nationwide problem, and, Dr. Rimm, you see the broad picture. Dr. Rimm, you promote working together with teachers, which is what parents really want; we just need more encouragement. I'm glad to see your thoughts in local newspapers but hope you'll be syndicated someday soon as parents are concerned everywhere and sure would benefit from your commonsense solution.

Concerned Parents

****

Disorganized Daughter

Dear Dr. Sylvia,

Our child is disorganized with keeping assignments turned in, misplacing objects such as her band instrument, keeping her room picked up, etc. We worry that this disorganization will intervene with what she wants to achieve. For example, she forgot to write a speech for Student Congress elections and, therefore, lost out. Is this a problem we should let her work out for herself, or should we take a more active role? She is very involved in extracurricular activities by her own choice and has little free time. She is 11 and in the sixth grade. I am at my wits' end.

Type A Dad with Type B Daughter

Dear Type A Dad,

The answers to your questions are yes and yes. Sometimes she will learn more by learning from consequences, as in the Student Congress elections. Your main role relative to such issues where consequences are most effective is to extend your genuine sympathy, e.g., "It's really too bad you lost that opportunity. I think you would have been a good representative."

You should take a more active and consistent role relative to homework and insist that she keep her room picked up. Room inspections on Friday night before weekend activities serve well as a reminder that reasonable order is expected as your daughter's share of home responsibilities. I emphasize "reasonable." Children shouldn't be expected to have perfect rooms. Since weekends are often times when visitors come, it is reasonable to expect your daughter to pick up clothes and toys by the weekend and organize herself for the week ahead before she becomes involved in any weekend social activities including television or friends. Be positive, firm, and fair at inspection time. She needs only to stay in her room until it bears some resemblance to order. Afterward, admire her skill at organizing herself, and tell her about the pleasure you feel when the whole house looks nice.

Friday can also be homework inspection day. Ask her teachers to provide you with an assignment report on Friday. My book *Underachievement Syndrome: Causes and Cures* has some samples you may use. As long as there tends to be missing assignments, all books should come home on Fridays. She can then make up all missing assignments before social fun begins. That may be a fairly large chore the first weekend or two, but she'll soon learn that if she gets her daily work done, weekends will be relaxing with no extra work to do. Setting up a regular daily homework time will help her form good habits and will prevent homework buildup.

Dad, don't start the homework and cleanup routine at the same time. Your daughter will feel overwhelmed. I'd suggest the school assignments as first priority. After that habit has improved, add the room inspection. One more suggestion—notice if disorganization is a conflict between you and your wife. If it is, it will be important that you are united in your organization expectations.

Incidentally, since your daughter is very involved in extracurricular activities, she may be more Type A than you think.

****

Daughter Unhappy in Cooperative Learning

Dear Dr. Sylvia,

Our daughter is in a cooperative learning classroom. She is always expected to teach the children that can't keep up with the class. She is becoming resentful and would rather pursue her own interests when she finishes her assignments. The teacher says this method is necessary to teach her to work with others. What can we do as parents? How can we make her feel better about the situation? We'd like our daughter to be learning in school, not just teaching.

Mom and Dad Who Value Learning

Dear Mom and Dad Who Value Learning,

Cooperative learning is sweeping the country. Like other educational fads, sometimes teachers take this one too literally and do "too much of a good thing." It *is* good for your daughter to have some experiences with teaching others as well as some group experiences, but she should also have many opportunities to learn either in groups and/or independently.

Explain to your daughter that teaching can be the highest form of learning. Encourage her to develop her own creative approaches to helping other children learn. Suggest that she keep a journal of new teaching approaches that work and that she share her journal with you and her teacher.

Without telling your daughter, make an appointment with her teacher and explain your daughter's frustration and your encouragement of her involvement so that her teacher knows that you are being supportive. Ask the teacher to suggest some independent projects that your daughter can do at home and school. I expect that her teacher will compromise with you and provide your daughter with both cooperative and independent learning. Hopefully, this teacher who believes in cooperative learning will understand your willingness to cooperate and will, in turn, cooperate with you.

Whether or not this last alternative is persuasive enough to your daughter's teacher, as parents you will want to organize some creative family learning opportunities at home. It is important that your daughter share with you a love of learning. If school does not seem appropriately challenging this year, and if you tried to communicate this respectfully to her teacher, your interesting home experiences will sustain her through this unchallenging year. Next year will undoubtedly be more interesting, and she will at least have learned a creative and respectful means of sustaining herself through some boredom.

****

Shy Daughter Doesn't Participate in Class

Dear Dr. Sylvia,

I have a daughter who started high school this fall. She's always been a very good student, and now a situation has developed in French class where she does very well on her tests, but her grade is falling down a lot because she doesn't participate in class. She's a very shy person, and I think she would rather fail than have to participate. I'm wondering if you have any suggestions for this situation.

Shy Mother

Dear Shy Mother,

It is difficult not to sympathize with your daughter's shyness since you know exactly how she feels. Nevertheless, an important part of learning a foreign language is learning to speak in that language, so the teacher has good reason to lower her grade for non-participation. I expect that she participates in other classes where speaking up doesn't feel as threatening. She probably worries that teachers or other students may make fun of any faulty pronunciation.

Suggest to your daughter that she practice her vocabulary and some simple French conversations on a tape recorder and then listen to herself once daily to see if she can improve her pronunciation. As she notices her own improvement, her confidence will grow. There are also prepared conversational tapes which will help her practice with appropriate French accent, and her teacher will probably be happy to give her some of those.

Perhaps she could muster the courage to volunteer an answer once each class period. That would be enough to communicate to her teacher that she is making an effort and would help her to experience some success.

Since you were shy, it would be easy to be too sympathetic to her problem. She is likely to assume that you believe her teacher is downgrading her inappropriately, and she may use your sympathy as an excuse to avoid this difficult challenge. Instead, you may want to let her know that you have had many similar feelings, and if she learns to concentrate on her French pronunciation instead of how others may be evaluating her, she will probably improve her language quite a bit. Please do emphasize to her that you're very sure that her teacher doesn't expect perfect pronunciation, but any teacher has a right to expect effort. If she overcomes this difficult hurdle, it will be an important preparatory step for college, which is not too far away.

****

Son Dependent on Punishments

Dear Dr. Sylvia:

My son has a strange school achievement pattern. Each year he looks forward to school and even seems to enjoy it. However, his first quarter report card always comes home with bad grades and low effort. The teachers usually tell us that he's a nice kid, but he doesn't do much work. We then read him the "riot act" and threaten to punish him if he doesn't put his act together. That seems to help. He works harder and gradually improves his grades. By the end of the year, he's doing fine but repeats the failure pattern at the beginning of the next year. He just won't get going unless we yell and scream. We're worried that he's going to depend on our punishments instead of his own motivation.

Tired of Screaming

Dear Tired of Screaming,

The beginning of each school year usually involves review of the past year's curriculum. Your son may believe he can handle the work effortlessly since it seems easy. His poor grades undoubtedly come from his much too casual approach to schoolwork, and he is probably as surprised as you by the low grades. Grades drop very quickly for children who do not hand in assignments.

Your serious message about school should come before school begins in the fall and need not involve threats or punishments. Instead, you and your son can set up a regular study time and place. A desk or table in a quiet room is appropriate. Don't let him convince you that he "must watch TV" while working. After his daily work is done, you or your husband should look it over to show your interest and concern. You don't actually need to correct it; leave that for his teacher. Take an interest in what he's learning. It is especially important that your husband tell your son he expects him to study and work hard. A serious "man-to-man" talk often helps.

Tell your son that you'll be calling his teacher after the first four weeks of school to ask about his progress. You can expect a more positive start with these early and direct homework and study expectations.

Apparently your son is capable of doing good work, but you're absolutely correct about your concern. We don't like children's school motivation to come from fear of punishment. A little early planning can prevent under-achievement. Although mothers are frequently the main message carriers about school for elementary-age boys, a father-to-son message is often more effective where a father is available. Incidentally, beginning the school year with regular study times and routines is a good pre-ventative technique for any other children in your family, even if they don't appear to have school problems.

****

Son Needs Study Skills

Dear Dr. Sylvia,

My concern is that my sixth-grade son is not going to have the study skills he will need in the years ahead. Everything has always come so easily for him; he never has to study at all. He also doesn't like to take the time to read his whole assignment, so he just scans the pages. He always gets great grades, so he doesn't think it is necessary.

Mom Who Is Worried
About The Future

Dear Mom Who Is Worried About The Future,

You have a legitimate concern although his teachers may be reassuring you that your son is doing well. The real problem comes from his assumption that since he gets good grades for doing little work, "smart" should mean learning comes easily. As the curriculum becomes more difficult, and learning takes more effort, he may indeed feel threatened and worry because he won't feel as intelligent. He may avoid challenging himself or meeting the higher standards of others since he may fear that more effort may not produce instant success and might make it appear that he isn't as intelligent as the reputation he's developed or not as smart as his parents expect. He could easily get into some avoidance habits like neglecting homework, handing in incomplete assignments, and ignoring responsibilities which appear difficult. These avoidance habits, grouped together, form Underachievement Syndrome.

I suggest you plan a conference with your son's teacher to discuss your observations and also to listen to hers. She may already be noticing his careless work in school. Perhaps together you can share some information about your son's special interests and provide some in-depth independent projects which he could choose to work on at home or in school. It might be good to label them "extra credit" projects and permit him to start with one of his choice. It would be good if his project resulted in a real product which he could share with his peers or with students older or younger than he. Although he is undoubtedly bright, don't assume that he can carry through the entire project on his own. He'll require guidelines for doing his initial research and also for his product construction. He'll need feedback from his teacher and/or parents at several steps along the way. He may work alone or with a small group of other students that the teacher feels could benefit from extra challenge.

Some examples of products may include a book, a musical composition, an art exhibition or mural, a science experiment beyond grade level, a stage or video production, a piece of sculpture, or a business or carpentry project. Of course, there are many other potential possibilities. Critical to the project should be planning, library research, step-by-step carry-through of the project, and evaluation by himself, his teachers, and in some cases, his peers. You can see that this kind of enterprise will permit your son to experience challenge, perseverance, and the success which comes from in-depth involvement.

****

College-Bound Senior Lacks Self-Esteem

Dear Dr. Sylvia,

Our daughter is a senior this year, soon to go on to college, at least five years for the field she has chosen. She is very intelligent, fast reader, etc., and was working several grades ahead until junior high. Since then she "doesn't want to be the smartest kid in her class but only wishes to have friends." So, it's been a constant struggle for honor roll. Her work isn't handed in, etc. One of her teachers said if she would find something to challenge her she might try. How can we help her to prepare for what's ahead?

I feel part of her problem is lack of self-esteem. If she doesn't do well she quits easily. Never learned how to work. Any insight would be greatly appreciated.

Mom Who Wants To Help

Dear Mom Who Wants To Help,

I think you are probably correct in your analysis of your daughter's problem—a lack of self-esteem. The peer pressure not to achieve may also be part of her problem, but it is more likely that she is using that as an excuse or defense. You're probably reassuring her by telling her she could get all *A*s if she only handed in her work. Oddly enough, that probably causes her more pressure. She probably thinks that you expect all *A*s. She may actually be afraid of the challenge the teacher thinks she wants. All her excuses may be created to protect her from her underlying fear that she is not as smart as she thinks she would like to be. I don't know enough about your daughter's abilities to tell for sure, but I have a great amount of confidence in a mother's observations.

Tell her that what counts most to you and her dad is her attitude. What really pays off in life is effort and hard work. Explain that the grade she gets is unimportant if you believe she is really working hard.

Also, let her know that it is easy to get *A*s in elementary school but much harder in high school and extremely difficult in college. All these messages give her permission to work hard without the worry that her hard work might not result in *A*s. Since she was a super student in elementary school, she may truly be afraid that she isn't as smart as she'd like to be.

Also, give her permission to be a nerd. Let her know (and I'm quoting a Rockford, Illinois, teacher) that *"the nerds of today own the Lamborghinis of tomorrow,"* and in college, no one cares if you were a nerd in high school.

This is your daughter's senior year, and there is probably very little you can do about her grades or her effort in high school; but college is ahead. If you let her know that extraordinarily hard work will be required, and you don't expect her to get all *A*s, you'll actually be reducing the pressure she feels. She is undoubtedly a highly intelligent young lady. However, the reality is that no matter how smart she is, there will be many others who are more intelligent than she. Also, no matter how smart she is, she will always wish she were smarter. Almost everyone feels that way at some times in their lives. She has probably decided that she is better at social life than at school. Unfortunately, while social expertise is an excellent asset, it is much more useful when combined with academic success.

Your own keen perception of her lack of self-esteem has probably guided you to reassuring her of how intelligent she is, which in turn has accidentally caused her more feelings of pressure. Why not "lay it on the line?" She is very bright, but so are lots of other kids. Fortunately, there's lots of room in the world for many intelligent persons but only providing they are willing to work hard.

Good luck. I know you really care.

****

19-Year-Old Son Terrified of Tests

Dear Dr. Sylvia,

How do you advise a 19-year-old son in a career direction? He's terrified of tests—even aptitude tests. He's also afraid of counselors. When will he learn to take tests and what can we do?

Tired of Parenting

Dear Tired of Parenting,

It sounds as if your 19-year-old is in great need of help but fearful of receiving any. You may want to do a little contacting of counselors for him. Find a counselor who will be willing to meet with him to establish rapport by talking to him first instead of testing.

Some counselors will be happy to change their usual procedure to accommodate your son. After the counselor knows him better, they can decide together whether testing is necessary.

Test anxiety is a common problem that can be helped. A combination of relaxation strategies and study skills seem to help young people adjust to the test-taking experiences they must cope with in their education.

By age 19, young people who have no sense of career direction can often make big strides once they're given the opportunity for help, but going for help appears to be a difficult hurdle for your son to jump. If he won't get career counseling, hard as it may be, you'll have to insist that he get some kind of job to support himself. Actually, regular work at a very boring job may be the best way to convince him that he'd prefer career counseling and a further education.

****

Will Underachiever Change in College?

Dear Dr. Sylvia,

If my son has always underachieved and he is now in college, can he survive? Will that underachieving be continued, or can he resolve to change that pattern and become successful?

Hopeful Mother

Dear Hopeful Mother,

There is good reason to be hopeful, but the "ball is now in his court." It is certainly good to know that he made it into college. Many underachieving students, though they are very capable, drop out of high school or don't even attempt college. Whether he reverses his underachievement now depends on many environmental issues, but mostly it depends on your son's resolve to do something about the problem.

For the most part, the peer pressure to underachieve changes in college to a peer pressure to achieve. If he befriends students who are immersed in learning rather than partying, that will surely be in his favor.

A role model, either as professor or employer, can be an inspiration to him. An achieving adult whom he admires can have a powerful impact on the direction of his college career. A strong or passionate interest in a subject or career direction can also be an important motivator.

Probably a most powerful influence on your son can be the "right" female friend. An achieving woman who admires and inspires him can help him to give his values a more mature perspective. His interest in achievement may then soar.

Of course negative influences, such as inappropriate peer groups or woman friends, can also expedite his dropping out of college. If he was an underachiever until college, he has much to learn including perseverance, study skills, and reasonable, rather than magical, goal setting.

Try to be optimistic and supportive in your conversations with your son. Encourage him to find tutoring or counseling if he feels he requires help. However, if he fails or drops out, the world of work and independence or the armed services provide disciplined environments where he can discover the pains of adult responsibility. After a few years of real-life struggles, many young people are happy to earn their way back to a higher education and value it much more after their struggle.

Mother, please be patient and kind but not so kind that you do too much for him. If he doesn't make it in college, invite him to live on his own and earn his own keep. Of course, keep an open invitation for Sunday dinner.

Underachievement and superachievement are often reverse sides of the identical coin. Some underachievers become very motivated and powerful achievers. For others, underachievement becomes a lifelong problem.

****

Drop-Out Dad

Dear Dr. Sylvia,

I'm a ninth-grade dropout, and I'm not ashamed of it. I've gone through life, and I've used my education very little except for reading, writing, and arithmetic. I've done about every job, and I've learned it from scratch. When I dropped out of school, we had a vocational school where we could simply go and take up a trade. I've raised three kids who dropped out of school. They learned in their own time. There was one teacher who was always on my son, and I hated him so bad because he'd call him stupid, mental, and idiot. He destroyed that kid's confidence, and that can tear a kid apart. High school wasn't right for me or my kids. Don't you think some kids are better off dropping out?

Proud To Be A Dropout

Dear Dropout,

I don't know for sure whether the quality of your personal life would have been better or different if you had continued through high school, but I don't think you can really know either. When you dropped out of high school, you closed many doors on opportunities which you will never know about.

It's very clear to me, however, that school was not a positive experience for you or your kids. While I don't

believe any teacher should call a student derogatory names, I can't help but wonder if your own negative attitude about school was passed on to your children. They may have attended school with the belief you've given them that school would be a waste of their time. As a result they probably made little effort, avoided learning, and may even have been disruptive.

Teachers choose their careers because they want to guide children in learning. They know they will encounter some discipline problems, but when students show no interest in learning and disturb the learning of others, teachers feel frustrated and angry and often direct their anger at the perpetrators of the disturbances. That isn't to justify the teacher's inappropriate language. However, it may not be the teacher's language that destroyed your son's self-confidence, but you, a well-meaning father with your message that school is a waste of time. I know you really cared and wanted your son to build confidence, but how can a son build any confidence in his ability to learn in school if his father doesn't value what he is doing in school?

It may be too late to do anything about this for your own children, but perhaps they may read my response and will give a more positive message about school to their children. Children gain so much more from a school environment if their parents believe that there is much that is important for them to learn in school. When they become learners and workers, their confidence grows dramatically.

As to your experience in vocational school, I do agree that vocational school can provide very relevant training after students have accomplished the learning of basic skills. However, a high school foundation provides many options for students, one of which is vocational. Since 15- and 16-year-olds don't often have the experience to know what career they will wish to pursue for the remainder of their adult years, a broader foundation gives them more choices. The narrowed training of vocational skills can restrict options too soon, although it can prepare students well once they are certain of their career direction.

Although you dropped out of high school, I hope you'll encourage your grandchildren to learn as much as possible in school and that you'll give them a clear message of respect for the teachers who are entrusted to give them the opportunities that your tax dollars pay for. There are so many countries in the world where children are so thankful for each day of learning. Encourage your grandchildren to value the important privileges and opportunities they have by telling them that school learning will be important to them for their entire life. I'm glad you "made it" successfully without high school, but society has become much more competitive. Job ads for factory work now include a high school diploma requirement or GED equivalent. The GED test is now more difficult than it was before. "Making it" without an education has also become much more difficult in our country today, and an adult without a high school diploma is at a great disadvantage. Don't give your grandchildren "an easy way out" by complaining about schools and teachers. They will want to learn only if you and their parents value their education. If they are successful in school, they are much more likely to be successful in life.

****

Perfectionistic Daughter is Slow Worker

Dear Dr. Sylvia,

My 15-year-old daughter is a slow, deliberate worker, but may not complete tasks. She's more concerned with accuracy and "getting it right." She doesn't like to be wrong and won't ask for help. How can I get her to "lighten up" and take pressure off herself?

Worried Mother

Dear Worried Mother,

Your daughter is perfectionistic and has a problem that many women and some men struggle with. Their inner pressure to be perfect can cause children much anxiety, can inhibit creativity, and can actually result in underachievement. Perfectionists often paralyze themselves with fear if they don't accomplish the impossibly high goals they set for themselves.

Ironically, perfectionism can result from too much praise and too much success. Children who do extremely well internalize a pressure to maintain that high performance. As they move to more difficult curriculum and more competitive environments, that becomes increasingly hard. While some students adjust to more realistic standards for themselves, some slow down for fear they will not be successful enough, and still others avoid school tasks entirely and make excuses because they fear they will not meet their new high standards. They tend to be very self-critical and don't accept criticism from others because their self-concepts are so fragile.

While high performance may cause children pressure, extreme praise may also have initiated the problem. Children enjoy the praise their parents give them, and praise *is* healthy for them. However, praise is a message to children of parental values and expectations. If you have given extreme praise such as perfect, the best, the smartest, brilliant, etc., it has communicated to your daughter that these are your expectations. When she finds she can no longer earn that high praise from you, she may feel praise-deprived and try to solicit more praise from you by putting herself down and encouraging your reassuring praise.

Now, what are the remedies for your perfectionistic adolescent? Praise her accomplishments moderately as in "that was good work," "you really persevere," "you're a good thinker, a good kid, a hard worker, etc." Be sure to encourage her father to give her moderate praise as well. Perfectionistic children are often "daddy's little girls."

Don't back away from occasionally criticizing, but criticize moderately and gently. Explain that she may or may not choose to accept your criticism, but ask her not to accept or reject it immediately but to take some time to think about your suggestions. She need not even tell you if she decides to accept it or not, but you want the opportunity to share your views. A caution: Criticize privately, not in front of others.

Most important, be a good role model for her. Be willing to accept your own flaws, and let her hear you talking about how hard that may be for you. Be sure she hears you acknowledging your own mistakes occasionally, and if her dad is perfectionistic, encourage him to let your daughter know how imperfect he may be.

Let her know that no matter how intelligent people are, they'd always like to be more intelligent, but that there is no such place as smartest, except temporarily.

Be sure there's time for fun and play and humor in the family. Humor and learning to laugh at oneself helps a great deal in overcoming the fear that one won't be perfect enough. Most important, don't pressure her by telling her that she is perfect. Nothing you can say will perpetuate the problem more than reassuring her she is perfect.

****

Family Relationships and Discipline

Uncommunicative Daughter

Dear Dr. Sylvia

My daughter is somewhat uncommunicative, and I often wish to know more about her thoughts, feelings, and needs. How can I encourage her to share important information with me and get beyond short "fine" answers?

Communicative Father

Dear Communicative Father,

I'm glad you're making an effort to communicate with your daughter because, first of all, it indicates how much you really care about her, and secondly, it is an extremely important learning experience for her. Your communication with each other forms a basis for her comfortable communication with males in the future.

I don't know from your question whether your daughter also has problems with mother-daughter conversation. If they do communicate well, and you don't, a dynamic, which I call "Father is an Ogre," may be taking place. In this ritual, the mother-daughter close relationship may be tied to the assumption that father is

too strict or father doesn't understand girls. The intimate mother-daughter relationship may thus be enhanced by secret communication which eliminates you from closeness to your daughter. Your wife may be engaging in this conspiratorial conversation with no intent to harm you or your daughter, but based on her belief that she wants to be open and honest with your daughter. Their closeness may have the impact of "leaving you out" and may be causing your daughter to believe that you don't really understand her. If you suspect this is the case, I suggest you share with your wife my book *How To Parent So Children Will Learn*, chapter 2, "The United Front."

Regardless of whether your daughter communicates well with your wife or not, here are some suggestions that will help you and her build a closer relationship:

1. Arrange to be her "driver" to a weekly activity when you and she can be in the car together with no one else, so there are no distractions or competition.

2. Talk to her about yourself and your own feelings. You may want to share with her some of your childhood experiences, some of your thoughts about your work or politics or religion, or about the *positive* qualities of your marriage or family life. Doing this will

model communication for her. However, under no circumstances should you "put down" her mother or siblings. Subtle "put-downs" may draw her closer to you temporarily, but will divide the family.

3. Tell your daughter how much you love her mother and how you met and courted her. That will bring you closer because you will be sharing your feelings.

4. You and your daughter may plan occasional surprise parties or gifts for other family members.

5. Plan a work project that you and your daughter can do together. A shared interest will make talking easier.

6. Consider taking a father-daughter trip. Either a day trip or weekend trip will give you more time to get to know each other. Your unique experience together will help cement your relationship and make communication easier.

7. Feel confident about talking in any style that makes you feel comfortable. Don't expect that your wife's guidelines or mine are the best ones. Our talk may feel stilted to you, and it's important that your communication feels natural to you.

8. Give yourselves plenty of time to build your relationship. Once your daughter begins talking more openly to you, expect to do your share of listening. Some of that may seem like boring listening, but that's an important investment to make for the daughter you so clearly love.

****

Absentee Dad Wants Relationship With Son

Dear Dr. Sylvia,

I was divorced from my wife. I went through some alcohol treatment and now, after about eight years, I'd like to be back in touch with my son, who is twelve. I've made some contact through a social worker and through my son's counselor. My son is saying, "Leave me alone. I really know my stepdad as my own dad. I'm really not interested in hearing any more from you, my natural dad." What's a good way for me to pursue this relationship and to be available to my natural son without interfering with his independence and creating a stir now that he is an adolescent?

Dad Who's Too Late

Dear Dad,

Yes, you are too late to become involved in your son's life as a typical father would be, and almost anything you arrange will disrupt the family life to which he's become adjusted. Actually you're "too late" involvement would be terribly unfair to your son, his mother, and his stepfather. It's only reasonable to live with the consequences of your earlier problems, although you have certainly earned your way back to a better life.

There is an important communication you could make to your son which would give him the opportunity to choose to get to know you when he wishes and would not interrupt his present life. You could write him a letter of apology for not being there when he needed you. You could explain the route you've taken to put your life back together and could let him know that you'd like to be a friend when and if he would ever like to meet with you. You'll want to explain that you agree that his stepfather, and not you, has earned the role of father and that you don't wish to establish yourself in his place. Also let him know that you will leave any further communication up to him but will always keep him informed of your whereabouts should he want to initiate any contact.

I'm sorry I don't have a happier answer for you. Loss of a son is truly a sad loss, but he will appreciate your love more if you don't interfere with his present life and leave any initiatives to him.

****

Kids Call Mom at Work;
Complain About Each Other

Dear Dr. Sylvia,

A problem that occurs every summer when my kids are home (now 14 and 16) is that they fight while my husband and I are at work. They call me and complain about the other. There is nothing I can do from where I am, and I'm frustrated and very concerned for the rest of the work day. Sometimes things have escalated to the point where I think they may kill each other. Any suggestions?

Working Mom

Dear Working Mom,

First let me assure you that your fighting children are not likely to kill each other. Sibling rivalry may get rather nasty, but it rarely approaches murder. It actually becomes much less of a problem when mother is not there to mediate. Fourteen- and sixteen-year-olds can escape to the solitude of their rooms if the going gets too rough.

First of all, tell your teenagers that they *absolutely* may not call you at work unless it is truly an emergency. Most bosses don't appreciate children interrupting their employees, although they would surely understand if it were an emergency. If your children misuse the emergency privileges, charge them for your time. Three dollars each time they make an unnecessary call should

minimize that telephone ringing and will keep you more efficient and more fair to your employer.

Fourteen- and sixteen-year-olds should have busy summers. Both are old enough to be working outside the home unless they have other planned activities. Mothers have a great need for babysitters during the summer, and both your children are of qualifying age. Sports, summer school, camp, art and music classes, or other structured activities are good alternatives for part of the summer. It sounds as if your two children are bored and don't understand the importance of your career. I notice that you don't mention their calling their father. Undoubtedly, neither he nor his boss would tolerate the calls, and neither should you. You and your husband take work seriously. You're good role models. It is now time to give a message about the importance of work to your children.

****

Angry, Disrespectful Daughter

Dear Dr. Sylvia,

My daughter is so angry and disrespectful. Although she used to be a good student at school, her grades are terrible now. Does anger and defiance play a big part in underachieving adolescents? Is it a symptom?

Disappointed Dad

Dear Disappointed Dad,

That passage from childhood to adulthood, known as adolescence, characteristically involves some pushing of limits and exploring of independence. However, if your daughter is very defiant and angry, it is likely that she is also an underachiever. If she's very rebellious at home, she may also be very rebellious at school. While that isn't always the case, it is a logical relationship. If she is busy fighting her parents, who obviously want her to achieve, she is likely to be battling teachers as well and avoiding doing the schoolwork her parents and teachers expect.

The anger and defiance are symptoms of your daughter's feelings of powerlessness. They don't necessarily mean that your daughter actually is powerless, but only that she feels that way. Her powerless feelings may be relative to her having had too much power too early, or they may be caused by your not giving her enough freedom and power for her age. It's strange how two opposite situations can cause the same symptoms, isn't it? You'll need to diagnose your own daughter to determine the cause, but the cure is pretty much the same and is fairly hard to accomplish.

Your role is to be sure that you and her mother are both fair and firm. The first is easier than the latter. Keep your limit setting reasonable and clear. Don't overpunish her, or she will become more rebellious. Be sure to keep a one-to-one positive relationship between you and her and her mom and her. Don't ever let her trap either of you into negative criticism about the other parent. (She will try, I promise you.) Let her know that you both love her, but hold onto fair limits and rules. Be very clear that you and your spouse consider academic achievement to be the very first priority. Don't give her specific grade expectations, but insist she work and study hard. You should both agree that her social life will be secondary and will depend on her completion of all homework responsibilities. Don't let her manipulate you out of that commitment.

If your daughter is angry and defiant, and you and your spouse can stay positive, patient, and firm, she and you are likely to survive. If you decide that either of you need counseling, choose a counselor that works concurrently with parents and their teenagers and will help you to guide her through precarious adolescence.

****

Working Mother as Role Model
for Daughter

Dear Dr. Sylvia,

I want my daughter to know that I work a lot of hours so that she can have the things she needs, but I don't want her to feel guilty about it, and I don't want her to think I'm away because I want to be. How can I be a good role model for her?

Industrious Mom

Dear Supermom,

You can be a wonderful role model for your daughter if she understands the real value of your work. Women didn't choose to join the work force only because they wanted to earn a salary. A salary is important, of course, to provide more for your whole family. However, even more important, let your daughter know that your work helps you to feel good about yourself and permits you to make a contribution to our society. Let her know that you take pride in doing quality work and in fully earning your salary. Explain that although you are tired, your weariness comes with the satisfaction of accomplishment.

Of course you miss her when you're working. All mothers feel some guilt about not being with their children. However, in your independence and responsibility,

you are fostering her independence and responsibility. She will respect you more because you value yourself. She will also gain confidence by taking responsibility for doing more for herself rather than depending on you to do for her.

Be sure she does her share of home chores so that she knows she is helping to make the extra material goods possible. Work as partners in some of these daily chores so that she doesn't feel punished because you work so much. Also, working together permits you to spend some valued one-on-one time as cheerful working partners. It will even provide some nice times for personal conversation.

Don't apologize to your daughter. Instead, tell her what a good role model you are and what important work you do. She'll take a new pride in your accomplishments and hers. However, Supermom, you must also put aside your work and find time for fun and laughter. Material possessions will never be a replacement for the fun you and your daughter should find time to share.

Most women, and some men too, struggle with the guilt of playing so many roles. Your guilt may not go away, but you will get better at managing it if you stop apologizing for it and pat yourself on the back instead. Incidentally, when your children have their own children and you become a grandmother, you'll again relive the stress of finding time for grandparenting and career.

Women wanted the opportunity to work outside the home. Combining work outside the home with family responsibilities is not easy, but we walk with our heads higher, and so will our daughters. Value what you accomplish and your daughter will too.

As to your daughter's feelings of guilt, don't worry about those. She should appreciate the efforts and sacrifices you make to give her the extras, and she shouldn't take your contributions for granted. On the other hand, if you don't exhibit guilt, she'll be unlikely to feel too much guilt and will value you as an ideal role model.

****

Sister Teases Younger Brother

Dear Dr. Sylvia,

I have a 15-year-old daughter and a 12-year-old son. Andrea enjoys teasing everyone in the family, including her brother, John, but it wears on her brother. He gets short-tempered and sometimes so angry that he hits her and is really violent. How can we handle this? Why can't they get along? They are both nice kids.

Mom, Tired of Fighting

Dear Mom,

Sibling rivalry is a natural part of family life, and if it doesn't show itself in some arguing or fighting, it will be exhibited in more subtle ways. However, the teasing and hitting you describe seems to have become a truly unpleasant ritual. Furthermore, teenagers can often be talked to about the problem. You have undoubtedly tried that already.

First, you will want to do some observation. Notice if Andrea's teasing is truly good-natured or if it is aimed directly at John's weak or vulnerable characteristics. If the first is true, you should have a one-to-one talk with John. If the second is the case, your personal tête-a-tête should be with Andrea. My guess is that Andrea will be your target and that she is attempting to maintain her "good girl, number one" status in the family. Here's a conversation you could try. Be sure to make it very personal and never within earshot of her brother or your spouse:

> *Andrea, we've always valued your kindness and sensitivity, and we even appreciate your teasing sense of humor. However, I've been noticing that the teasing you're doing with John doesn't sound like the kind person you really are. You're really targeting the very problems that John is trying to work on. Furthermore, the teasing isn't even terribly funny. I guess I can't*

really blame John for getting angry. What's even worse is that your mean teasing is getting to be a habit. I'm afraid you'll find yourself teasing your friends in the same way, and you won't even realize you're hurting them. I just don't think that's the real you. I'd really like it if I could help you to get over this bad habit because kindness is a quality I've always valued in you. We could even practice some nice things to say that would help John to feel better about himself.

Here's a sample personal conversation for John if the teasing is humorous and not mean, and he is truly overreacting. This conversation should not take place right after the incident, but at a calmer time:

John, I know it really gets to you when Andrea teases you, and in a sense, she knows just the buttons to push to get you into trouble. When you hit her, of course, we have to take her side because we can't encourage your violence, and we really want you to grow up to be a gentleman. So in a sense, she wins every time you lose your temper. Also, I worry that your bad temper at home might start happening with friends at school, and that will surely cause you many more serious problems.

Here are some suggestions you might try. You may have some more. After you try some of these, we could talk about how they worked or you could invent some new ones:

1. *You could notice how your dad and I respond to Andrea's teasing and try some of Dad's or my techniques.*

2. *You could take a walk or go into another room every time she teases. Either act "cool" as if you don't care, or if you're angry inside, take a run outside or punch your pillow behind your closed door so she doesn't even know she has gotten to you.*

3. *You could try saying something really nice to her. I know you're really sensitive and kind, and she might not know how to accept a compliment at first, but after you've said something nice to her a few times, she might even decide it's her turn to return a nice compliment.*

John, let's take a walk on Saturday, and you could let me know which ideas you've tried or if you've thought of any more.

As you can tell, this approach will work better with teenagers. If you're having problems with younger children, there are other suggestions in my book *How to Parent So Children Will Learn.* Whether it's teenagers or younger children, the more you mediate between them, the more they'll argue for your attention and try to get you on their side. These simple conversations are used to put you in an alliance with them without making their sister or brother appear to be the lesser sibling.

****

Maintaining Long-Distance Relationship With Teenager

Dear Dr. Sylvia,

I've been divorced for about 11 years, and my daughter has moved about 2000 miles away. She comes to visit in summer for a month and for a week at Christmas. In between, I try to telephone, but because she's now a teenager, I end up talking to her answering machine. When I am finally able to talk to her, I find myself going to the same dialogue—"How are you?" "I love you," "I care about you," "What's happening in

your life?" Communicating with a teenager is difficult at best, but more so when she's 2000 miles away. I'm wondering if you can give me any tips to get her talking so that I can feel more a part of her life.

Devoted Dad

Dear Devoted Dad,

All your conclusions about teenage conversation are correct when you're not there with her to just hang around and listen. Actually, teenagers can be quite verbal with adults if you're able to invest the time that it takes to build their trust and to establish rapport. Long-distance telephone calls are not very effective for that kind of conversation.

It would be good to try writing letters. They permit you to update her on what you're doing for work and fun, the latest movies or TV shows you've seen, or teenagers with whom you come into contact that remind you of her. In a letter, you can share stories about your own teenage years including school interests, sports, or college stories. Each topic you discuss in your letter has the potential for being used as a reference point for her answer to you. The more extensive your letters are, the more interesting hers will become. You may even want to include pictures or a funny joke or cartoon. Ask her to save your letters so that many years from now she'll have remembrances of your long-distance relationship, and send her a very special box in which to store them.

A letter every two or three weeks, whether or not she answers, will be enough to establish the closeness you'll want on the telephone.

Now when you call her, you'll have a bond that will permit better conversation. She'll soon be telling you about her boyfriends, and if you've shared some of your dating experiences, she may even ask your advice. Become involved in her interests and plan some events or trips for summer and Christmas vacation which involve her early input. She'll look forward to these and will enjoy the planning with you.

There is, of course, one important taboo. Never, under any circumstances, make any negative statements about her mother or her mother's friends. They may seem to help establish rapport at first, but will instead build a wall between you and your daughter eventually.

It is good to hear that you are devoted to your daughter and that you're persistent in your positive efforts at communication. It will help her in relating to other men in the future and will heal the hurts she probably feels due to her parents' divorce.

****

Social and Emotional

Peer Pressure in Middle School

Dear Dr. Sylvia,

How do you keep a smart boy from following peer pressure in middle school?

Powerless Parents

Dear Powerful Parents,

In many communities, middle school is the most difficult time for students who are capable of excellent achievement. From about fifth grade through ninth grade, there is a peer message to be cool, casual, and not too intellectual. Special vocabulary which labels students who appear too studious has varied through generations. Brain, nerd, schoolboy (or girl), bookie, and geek are the uncomplimentary terms used to describe serious students who do not fit in with the popular crowd. Each year I see preadolescents in my Clinic who are teased cruelly and even physically abused by groups of other students who will not accept the personality and interest differences of those who seem to care little about social life but are serious about learning. The serious student often feels lonely and unacceptably different.

Parents experience pressure too. They want their children to be true to their abilities and to set standards

of individuality and independence but fear for the loneliness their children may be experiencing. Just last week, a fifth-grade boy sat in my office and explained the "customs" that fifth graders were expected to adhere to including special ways to wear socks, ways to sit and not to sit, appropriate food to eat at lunch, and of course, appropriate standards of casualness. He said he didn't want to "do" the customs, but he was afraid the kids would beat him up if he didn't as they had his friend. Nor was he willing to let me talk to the teacher about the pressured activity.

You can't keep your child from feeling pressure in most middle schools unless you encourage him or her to conform to an antilearning standard. I see this as your opportunity to give your son a powerful message about independence and moral strength. Although it is difficult for you to watch him struggle to maintain values of integrity, honesty, individuality, and love of learning, these are values which will begin to "pay off" for him in only a few more years. Some helpful messages that teachers and counselors have shared with me follow:

1. Explain that the "nerds of today will own the Lamborghinis of tomorrow."

2. Explain that after Grade 12, no one cares who was popular in middle or high school.

3. Here's a "what do you call" joke to try:

Counselor: What do you call a student who studies hard, talks to the teacher after class, does extra work, does more than expected, and wants to do his/her schoolwork?

Student: Nerd, brain, geek.

Counselor: What do you call a man who works hard at his job, does more than expected, wants to meet high standards, and is interested in his work?

Student: Gee, I don't know.

Counselor: You call him "boss."

Let your children know that it will "pay off" to be strong despite peer pressure. Help them search out other students who share similar values so that they don't feel so alone. Encourage their involvement in positive school activities where they can share fun learning with other students—activities such as band, drama, forensics, computer club, school newspaper, Future Problem Solving, etc. Your son's positive involvement will help him through the peer-pressured days of middle and high school. Usually, by eleventh grade the negative peer pressure diminishes.

****

Daughter Withdraws From Using Abilities

Dear Dr. Sylvia,

My daughter seems to withdraw from using her talents and abilities because she doesn't want to show up her classmates. How can I encourage her to express rather than stifle herself?

Disappointed Mother

Dear Disappointed Mother,

From about fifth grade on, there is considerable peer pressure on preadolescents and teenagers to "fit in" with the popular crowd and be accepted by peers. This pressure often seems more extreme for females than it does for males, although most kids experience some conflict. On the one hand, they'd like to excel in their activities; on the other hand, they are not certain if their excellence will be acceptable to their particular group of friends. They often find themselves torn between developing their talents and hiding those same abilities and efforts for the sake of acceptance.

Girls who are extremely attractive and boys who are excellent athletes sometimes have enough status to manage to both excel and fit in. However, since teenagers rarely have a great deal of social confidence, hiding one's talents is a fairly frequent behavior. Parents such as you often look on with shock and disbelief as they see their children's talents going to waste and wonder if their adolescents will be able to recover their skills and confidence when they move on to young adulthood.

The answer to that difficult question varies depending on the individual adolescent, school environment, family, and peer group, so I can't really give you a definitive answer for your daughter. I assume you have already talked to her about the value of her abilities and the importance of peer independence. Hopefully, so have her teachers. There are often some peers and adults who may be especially effective in helping your daughter develop her abilities.

I can't tell by your question what your daughter's special abilities are. Teachers or professionals who have developed talents in those areas in which she excels can often be especially inspirational. For example, if science is a strength, a female scientist might be a real encouragement. If music is one of her talents, a band, orchestra, or choir director may be able to foster her interest. A school mentorship program is frequently extremely helpful for young people.

Summer specialty programs do much to promote positive peer interest in drama, art, music, computers, foreign languages, creative writing, business, science, or the environment. When adolescents are involved in high-interest activities, they frequently meet both peers and adults who share their interests and foster positive commitments.

Biographical literature provides stories of wonderful models of individualism and are highly effective for students who enjoy reading. My book *Gifted Kids Have Feelings Too* was written especially for the purpose of encouraging adolescents toward independence and achievement. Appropriate movies or video tapes may also be helpful.

Most important, try to provide a strong family learning and fun environment. Adolescents who see their parents as interested *and* interesting are much less vulnerable to the peer pressures that surround them.

****

Daughter Choosing Wrong Friends

Dear Dr. Sylvia,

How do you handle a situation in which you feel your child (12-year-old girl) is starting to choose the wrong friends? (Example: Friends encouraging the child to lie to parents, treat other children cruelly, make fun of others, and have a belligerent attitude.) What can I say to my child? Is it OK for me to discourage this strongly, or do I give my child a choice by giving examples? This is affecting school.

Powerless Mother

Dear Powerful Mother,

You are only as powerless as you believe you are, and I suggest that you believe in yourself and continue to use the power you have. Your power will decrease each year as your daughter progresses through adolescence. Your daughter is not too old to accept your limitations to her friendships, and these are critical times for parents to give their children guidelines on how to choose friends.

Make it clear to your daughter that quantity of friends or popularity are shallow values. Let her know that she can be strong enough to walk school corridors independently. Share with her that you value friendships, but that she should choose carefully. She should value herself sufficiently so that she need not join a group only because they have invited her. Suggest that she be particular and that she choose friends based on shared values and interests, kindness, and sensitivity. If she doesn't immediately find such friends, ask her to be patient. "Good" friends are more important than "more" friends.

Since your daughter has already befriended someone with inappropriate values, let her know that you disapprove. While it will be fine for her to be friendly to this girl in school, explain that she is an inappropriate friend to bring home or to visit. If your family believes in honesty, kindness, sensitivity, and respect, you are not required to apologize to your daughter for upholding these values. You can let her know that if her friend changes her values, you won't object to the friendship, but that you reserve the right as parents to guide her toward good values.

Don't worry if your daughter experiences temporary loneliness. It will build her character. Reassure her that she can survive well with loneliness, but friends with bad values will pull her down to their level. Even adults are affected by their adult friends.

Be sure to keep family fun going, and when your daughter asks to invite appropriate friends to your home, encourage her. Also encourage her to stay involved in positive school activities where she is more likely to relate to young people with better values.

Good luck. This is not an easy assignment. It is difficult to insist that your children be selective in their friendships.

****

TV in Adolescent's Room

Dear Dr. Sylvia,

My son has been begging to have a television in his room. We just got a new TV for our living room and now have a spare one we could give him. My husband doesn't like the idea because he's afraid he will watch too much. I think it would be good to let him choose his own programs, but I'm not sure. What do you think? He's a good kid.

Mom, Trying to be Fair

Dear Too Fair Mom,

I don't believe children or teenagers should have TVs in their rooms for multiple reasons. As a matter of fact, I feel so strongly about that issue that I wish all teenage in-room televisions would self-destruct immediately. You might even help that to happen. Television, at best, can be a nice family activity which includes some interludes for family laughter and conversation. Sometimes, parent interpretation or discussion is even appropriate. Certainly, television can be shared entertainment.

Bedroom television isolates adolescents from their families. It distracts children from homework, hobbies, and books. Most seriously, by high school age, it often becomes a sleep robber. Kids often tune into nighttime talk shows or films and spend important rest time watching absorbing programs, which add little to their well-being but leave them sleep-deprived and drowsy. They easily become "hooked" on nighttime television and quickly assume that they are "night people." Their biological rhythms change to fit their habit, and rising for school becomes more difficult. Dozing at their desk or staring dazed out the window becomes their school routine. Daytime alertness becomes part of the past. They watch television while the world sleeps and sleep while their fellow students learn.

Mom, I hope I have convinced you, while it may feel fair to give your son his own television since he is a "good kid," it is a risky plan. Even if he wished to earn the money for his own television, I don't believe he should be allowed to keep it in his room. I can be convinced about playroom, family room, kitchen, or adult bedroom, but absolutely not about children's or adolescents' bedrooms. I vote for destroying a television rather than risking it destroying your child. As to your husband's instincts about the issue, give him a hug and congratulate him on his good advice.

****

14-Year-Old Son Beginning to Lie

Dear Dr. Sylvia,

We have a 14-year-old boy, and I'm hoping that it's not too late for him. He's basically been a great kid and a fun kid to be with, but he's in high school and starting to be with different people and is being presented with some new situations. What we're finding is he's starting to push his limits to the point where he's lying to us about where he is and who he's with because he knows we wouldn't approve. When he's caught in his stories and lies and we confront him, he says, "Well, I didn't tell you because I knew that you wouldn't let me go." We're losing a lot of trust in him that we used to have. Is it effective at all when this happens to take some privileges away from him now, like grounding him or limiting certain things, or will that make him want even more to go against us?

Helpless Parents

Dear *Helpful* Parents,

You've done a good job raising your child until now, and I think you're saying that you feel helpless although you want so much to be helpful at this time. It sounds as if your son may have become involved with a crowd of kids whose values don't agree with yours. That's not uncommon in our society today, and it seems to be increasingly difficult to get kids through a safe adolescence, so don't be too quick to fault yourself for the changes you're seeing in your son.

You'll first want to examine the guidelines you've set for your son to decide if they are too strict or if they give him the reasonably increased freedom a high school student should expect. Think particularly about the times he's lied to you. Were his activities unsafe or inappropriate? If the activities were all right, you may be limiting him too much, and you may wish to expand his freedom a little more. More likely, they were inappropriate. Either way, you as parents will wish to set an outline plan for your son and then include him in the setting of firm and simple rules. You may feel pressured to give in on some issues, but he too will have to make some compromises. Lying is clearly unacceptable and can only lead to further mistrust, so you will want to be very firm about establishing that premise.

At very least, a 14-year-old should be letting his parents know where he is, should not be in other teenagers' homes unless parents are at home and should not be involved in smoking, drinking, and/or drugs. You as parents may want to establish some more stringent guidelines or some special situations where your son can have more freedom.

Don't overdo the punishments. Too many cause more anger and rebellion and do little to improve behavior. Do hold on to limits and agree to a fair consequence for lying so that your son can again earn trust.

When you consider the potential negative consequences you can use for teenagers, you'll soon realize you're somewhat limited and will run out of controls if you overuse them. Withholding money, telephone privileges, social outings, and driver's license use comprise the entire list. Thus, positive expectations and trust are more effective than punishment as long as you can use them. If you decide to use "grounding" (withholding all social privileges), one important weekend night is probably about all you and he can tolerate, and grounding for anything more than one weekend usually encourages the teenager to dig his heels in further and rebel.

Once you and your son agree to the limits and reasonable consequences, write down your agreement in a simple way and stay with it. Definitely include a negative consequence for any lying, and firmly hold to it despite your son's indication that it is either unfair or he doesn't care. Don't add to the punishment or renig on your commitment. Be sure that you, as parents, stay united. The worst problems are caused if your son learns he can manipulate one parent against the other. In that way, life will become a little more predictable for your son. Stay as positive and consistent as possible, and let your son know that you want to trust him. As he earns your trust, you'll be able to increase his freedom.

****

FURTHER READING

Davis, G. A., & Rimm, S. B. (2nd. Ed.) (1989, 1985). *Education of the gifted and talented.* Englewood Cliffs, NJ: Prentice-Hall, Inc.

Rimm, S. B. (1986). *Underachievement syndrome: Causes and cures.* Watertown, WI: Apple Publishing Company.

Rimm, S. B. (1990). *How to parent so children will learn.* Watertown, WI: Apple Publishing Company.

Rimm, S. B. (1990). *Gifted kids have feelings too.* Watertown, WI: Apple Publishing Company.

ARTICLES*

Rimm, S. B. (1984, Jan./Feb.). Underachievement...Or if God had meant gifted children to run our homes, she would have created them bigger. *G/C/T*, 26-29.

Rimm, S. B. (1988, May/June). Popularity ends at grade 12! *Gifted Child Today, 11*(56), 42-44.

Rimm, S. B., & Lovance, K. J. (1992, March/April). How acceleration may prevent underachievement syndrome. *Gifted Child Today*, 9-14.

Rimm, S. B., & Lovance, K. J. (in press). The use of subject and grade skipping for the prevention and reversal of underachievement. *Gifted Child Quarterly.*

*Reprints of articles are available upon request from Educational Assessment Service, Inc., W6050 Apple Road, Watertown, WI 53094.

For additional books, cassette tapes, and miscellaneous items by Sylvia B. Rimm, complete the order form on reverse side.

BOOKS:

Underachievement Syndrome: Causes and Cures $15.00

Guidebook for Underachievement Syndrome: Causes and Cures . . . 35.00

How to Parent So Children Will Learn 15.00

Sylvia Rimm on Raising Kids 15.00

Gifted Kids Have Feelings Too 15.00

Exploring Feelings 15.00
A Discussion Book for
Gifted Kids Have Feelings Too 15.00

Education of the Gifted & Talented
by Gary A. Davis & Sylvia B. Rimm 56.00

TAPE SETS:

Underachievement Syndrome: Causes and Cures (set of 6) 60.00

How to Parent So Children Will Learn (set of 3) 30.00

Gifted Kids Have Feelings Too (set of 2) 20.00

Educating Gifted Children (set of 2) 20.00

MISCELLANEOUS:

Q-Cards:

Parent Pointers 16.00

Student Stepping Stones 12.00

Teacher Tips 12.00

Learning Leads (set of all 3) 35.00

Newsletter: *How to Stop Underachievement*
Individual Yearly Subscription (4 Issues) 15.00

TESTING MATERIALS:

Specimen Sets:

Group Inventory for Finding Creative Talent (GIFT) 12.00

Group Inventory for Finding Interests (GIFFI) 12.00

Preschool and Kindergarten Interest Descriptor (PRIDE) 12.00

Achievement Identification Measure (AIM) 12.00

Group Achievement Identification Measure (GAIM) 12.00

Achievement Identification Measure -
Teacher Observation (AIM-TO) 12.00

EDUCATIONAL ASSESSMENT SERVICE, INC.
W6050 Apple Rd., Watertown, WI 53098-3937

TO ORDER BY PHONE:
Call 800/475-1118 or 414/261-7928, 8 to 3 CST, Monday-Friday
FAX 414/261-6622

® MasterCard   ® VISA

Name _____

Address _____

City _____ State _____ Zip _____ Phone ( ) _____

☐ Check enclosed payable to: Educational Assessment Service, Inc.
☐ Purchase order enclosed
☐ Charge to: ☐ VISA   ☐ MasterCard

Card # ☐☐☐☐☐☐☐☐☐☐☐☐☐

Expiration Date ☐☐

SIGNATURE _____

CATALOG NUMBER	DESCRIPTION	QUANTITY	UNIT PRICE	TOTAL PRICE
			Subtotal	
			Shipping / Handling	

Subtotal	
WI residents add * 5% sales tax	
TOTAL	

SHIPPING AND HANDLING CHART

SUBTOTAL AMOUNT . . ADD		
$20 or less $3.00	Over $200 . . . . 5%	
Over $20 to $200 . . . . . 10%	Outside Continental US 25%	
	(Over $200 . . . . .10%)	

All orders are normally shipped within 48 hours. In the event of any undue delay, you will be notified.

- Prices are subject to change without notice.
- All payments must be made through US banks or by international money order.
- Billings are NET 30 days, sorry, no C.O.D. orders.

- Orders requesting delayed billing will be held for shipment until the billing date requested.
- Our Customer Service Department must receive written notice of any problems within 30 days of receipt of your order.
- Materials returned in unusable and damaged condition will be appropriately billed.

*Eff. 4/1/94, in Wis. add 5.5%.